KEW COATS AND SCIMITARS

To Jill & Greg —
I hope you enjoy this story
of your great-grandfather!
Patty Kittel

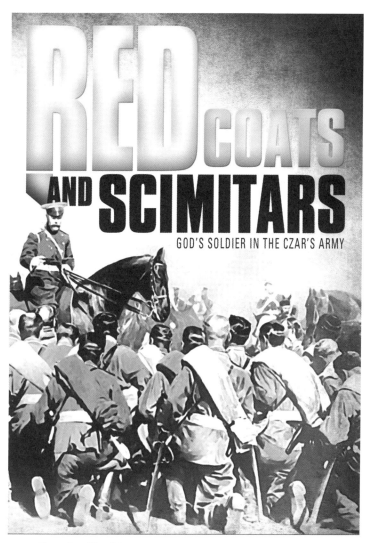

RED COATS AND SCIMITARS

GOD'S SOLDIER IN THE CZAR'S ARMY

PATTY KNITTEL

Pacific Press® Publishing Association

Nampa, Idaho | Oshawa, Ontario, Canada
www.pacificpress.com

Cover design by Steve Lanto
Cover design resources retrieved from Wikimedia Commons
Inside design by Kristin Hansen-Mellish

Copyright © 2014 by Pacific Press® Publishing Association
Printed in the United States of America
All rights reserved

The author assumes full responsibility for the accuracy of all facts and quotations as cited in this book.

Additional copies of this book can be obtained by calling toll-free 1-800-765-6955 or by visiting http://www.adventistbookcenter.com.

Library of Congress Cataloging-in-Publication Data:

Knittel, Patty, 1957–
  Red coats and scimitars / Patty Knittel.
     pages cm
  ISBN 13: 978-0-8163-5701-7 (pbk.)
  ISBN 10: 0-8163-5701-3 (pbk.)
  1. Schwartz, Karl, 1870–1953—Juvenile literature. 2. Seventh-day Adventists—Russia—Biography—Juvenile literature. I. Title.
  BX6193.S39K55 2015
  286.7092—dc23
  [B]
                                                  2014040444

October 2014

Dedication

I dedicate this book to my wonderful husband, Monty, who is the great-grandson of Karl Schwartz. Your heritage has been an inspiration to me—your encouragement and support my mainstay.

Acknowledgments

Thanks and credit go to Colleen Duty, Leslie Goodwin, Glenn Edgerton, and Dennis LeMaster for their research on the Schwartz family history and for gleaning stories from family members over the years. I'll always remember Colleen's excitement at finding the ship's manifest showing Karl Schwartz and his family coming to the United States.

Contents

1 A New Czar
11

2 Retribution
17

3 Young Love
24

4 All Grown Up
31

5 Hopes and Dreams
36

6 Sabbath
43

7 Against the Norm
47

8 Proposal
50

9 What God Hath Joined Together . . .
55

10 In the Service of the Czar
59

11 Sad News
62

12 The Imperial Guard
66

13 A Time to Celebrate
68

14 Plans
71

15 Escape
75

16 Red Coats and Scimitars
78

17 Walter and Anna
82

18 Home
87

19 A New Home
90

20 Land of Freedom
93

Epilogue
95

1
A New Czar

Beginning in 1763, a great migration of German settlers found a new life full of promise and reward in the expanding lands controlled by Russia. Catherine the Great was looking for a way to settle the areas that her country had recently conquered. Her admiration for the German people's work ethic and ability to make their land productive gave her an idea that led to a bold move. She sent word to the oppressed people in Germany and Poland, offering land, freedom of religion, and exemption from taxes and military service, along with a stipend to help them become established in her country.

The bravest ones who took a chance on this more-than-you-could-ask-for offer sent word back to others, who soon flocked to the Ukraine, southwest of Russia—at that time a country about the size of New Hampshire. These migrations continued into the mid-1800s until new Russian leadership gradually brought them to a halt. The Schwartz family was among the immigrants.

The Schwartzes lived in the village of Volhynia, between Chernobyl and Kiev, at the time of Czar Alexander II's death. The population of most villages at this time numbered about five hundred to a thousand, including children. The farm plots, between forty and eighty acres, were outside the villages. Some were a half-day's ride away. Those who held rights to plots closer to the village had usually been in the area the longest. It was common during planting and harvesting season for a family to spend the week out at the plot working from dawn until dusk, returning to their homes on Friday to bake, do other chores, and go to church on Sunday.

1881

Eleven-year-old Karl picked up another large, potato-sized rock and placed it with the others in his upturned leather apron. He had enough to make a trip to the pile. His younger brother, Julius Jr., met him there with a smaller load. The rocks tumbled down the growing pile with a clatter. Piles of these "plow-wreckers" could be seen at the end of every few rows, as high as the tallest boy could toss them.

Karl and Julius walked back to follow their father and the oxen. Their younger brother, John, was more interested in throwing dirt clods. "Come on, John! You're big enough to help with the rocks. We need to get this field plowed before dark today," Herr Julius Schwartz Sr. called.

The long winter season had finally given way to the warmer days of spring. The gradual disappearance of the low winter mist that continually hugged the flat hills brought a renewed sense of hope to the German immigrants—hope for a long growing season and subsequent abundant harvest.

Karl took off his *hut* (pronounced *hoot,* meaning "cap") to wipe the sweat from his forehead. "Look!" he yelled. "Someone's coming to see us." Everyone stopped in his tracks to gaze at a horse and rider cantering from the direction of town. They seldom had visitors when out in the field, a mile from town.

"Look, Father! Who could it be?" cried John, the seven-year-old.

Father clicked his tongue at the oxen and brought them to a stop. Shielding his eyes from the sun, he saw the rider approaching at a comfortable pace. This was a good sign that there was no emergency, but it was still a rare sight.

Tying the oxen to the plow, Father said, "Well, well. Let's go see who is coming. We needed a little break anyway."

Needing no more convincing, Karl, Julius, and John took off running in the direction of their campsite, stopping more than once to help John back to his feet after he tripped in the freshly turned earth. Father Julius soon caught up with them and beat them to the edge of the field.

They recognized the rider, Edvard, the son of their local schoolmaster. He waved as he turned into the gate of the Schwartz farm plot. He rode bareback, his legs flopping out at the sides with each trot.

"Greetings, Edvard! To what do we owe this honor?" Julius Schwartz Sr. took the reins of the young man's horse as he dismounted.

"*Danke,* Herr Schwartz. Father sent me to tell you the latest news from the capital since you won't be home for a few more days. This morning we heard from a villager who just returned from Kiev—the czar was assassinated a week ago!" Edvard, twelve years old, seemed pleased to be trusted with such important news.

"*Ach,* how did this happen? Who did such a thing?"

"They say some revolutionaries hid a bomb in an Easter cake and gave it to Alexander one morning as he left the palace. The bomb went off as the carriage rolled down the street. The czar bled to death after his leg was blown off!"

Shaking his head in disbelief, Julius Sr. muttered, "Will the bloodshed never end? They have tried many times to kill this man and have finally accomplished their goal. True, the Romanov czars aren't always the best rulers, but at least Alexander seemed to have the common man in his thoughts."

"So, is his son the czar now?" asked Julius Sr.

"Yes. Alexander the Third is now the czar."

"What does this mean, Father?" Karl asked, trying to sound grown up. "Will things be better for the people?"

"My father says it can only mean we have more hard years ahead of us," interrupted Edvard. "He says we need to pray for the new czar and his men."

"Your father is wise, Edvard. We appreciate very much your coming all the way out here to bring us the news. Now, won't you come and have lunch with us and rest a bit before you ride back to the village?"

"Thank you, sir. I'd like that very much." Edvard walked his horse over to the corral fashioned out of an array of sticks woven through larger posts driven into the ground. It looked somewhat like a large basket sitting next to the small living quarters on one corner of the property. Removing the bridle, Edvard led the mare inside.

"Karl, run out and untether the oxen and hobble them," directed Herr Schwartz.

"Yes, Father. Edvard, don't tell anything until I get back," Karl called over his shoulder.

They walked toward the smell of lunch wafting in the breeze while Herr Schwartz pondered the news and the czar's role in their lives. It was hard to understand the implications of what Edvard had shared. Life had been fairly predictable for the last twenty years.

Frau Juliana Schwartz looked up from her lunch preparations of potato soup and *brot* (meaning "bread") to see her men arriving. They lived in a tent during the planting and harvesting seasons.

"Welcome, Edvard. So good to see you," she said. "You must be hungry."

"Yes, Frau Schwartz."

"Come—have a seat."

Karl returned from the field huffing and puffing, but happy that Edvard's timing might mean an extra-long lunch break and an early meal. As Karl brushed dirt off his brown wool pants, he stomped his boots.

Their five-year-old sister, Emma, helped her mother by setting the makeshift table of planks for her parents, three older brothers, and her younger sister, Mathilda, who was three. Two-year-old Pauline sat on her mother's lap, and Frau Juliana hoped baby Henry would sleep through the commotion of people eating and visiting outside the tent.

A New Czar

As everyone settled down to enjoy the food on their plates, Herr Schwartz asked, "So, what do people think of this change in czars? What will it do to our already slow economy?" He passed the bowl of potato soup with his big hands.

Edvard quickly swallowed the soup in his mouth and replied, "No one's quite sure what to think yet. My father says he is a good husband and father to his wife and children, but we must wait and see what kind of leader he is for his people."

"Does anyone know the new czar's perspective on land and religion?"

"I don't know, sir," Edvard shrugged.

"Well, our status in this country since the colonial law was revoked ten years ago certainly couldn't get any worse. As long as they don't take our land and our religion away from us, we'll be fine."

"Father, would they really take our land?" Julius asked, looking worried.

"Not if I have any say in things. But I am just a man. We must pray for God's protection. He can change a czar's mind."

Mother handed Edvard more *brot*. "Edvard, tell me, how are your mother and sister?"

"Very well. Mother said to say Hello to you. She looks forward to your coming back to town."

"Well, that should be within the week," the elder Julius said as he pushed away from the table. Placing his *hut* firmly on his head, he stood up, resting his hand on Karl's shoulder.

"We mustn't let the sun go down before we get that field finished, boys. So, Karl, you and Julius clean up your places and go on ahead to hook up the oxen. We will be along shortly."

"Oh, Father, can't Edvard stay a little longer?" Karl pleaded.

"I have to get back to do my chores, Karl." Edvard's tone reminded Karl of his own father's firm directions.

"Oh, OK. Then I'll see you at church Sunday."

Karl and Julius headed for the stream to rinse off their dishes. Mother would heat water and wash them better later.

"Thank you for the delicious meal, Frau Schwartz! I always like to come at mealtime to get some of your cooking!"

"You can come every day if I get to hear compliments like that, young man! You tell your mother Hello for me too. Oh, and come by when we get home in a few days and get some apples, won't you?"

"I'll do that. See you Sunday!"

As Edvard walked toward the corral, Julius quietly pondered to his wife, "I wonder how much longer we will be able to meet together on Sunday with this news of the czar, *meine* Frau."

She nodded. "Oh, Julius, I hate to think of what could happen."

"I didn't want to worry the children, but I do fear for the future," he replied, frowning.

They clasped hands for a moment as they watched the boys walk back out to the field.

2 Retribution

Although the Orthodox Church held a strong influence over the religion of the country, the German immigrants were allowed to follow their own beliefs at this time, be it Lutheran or Reformed Baptist, or others.

There was a shortage of pastors, however, because of the many villages spread throughout the territory. Therefore, each congregation could expect to see its pastor only about every six weeks. Between the pastor's visits, the local schoolmaster would preside over the church service and any prayer meetings during the week. He was not allowed to "preach" per se but would read from a sermon book called the Predigtbuch. The people often felt they got more out of this book than they did from the sporadic sermons from the pastor!

The whitewashed wooden church seemed fuller than usual the next Sunday as the Schwartz family members—all nine of them—found their way to the wooden pew everyone knew was theirs. Schoolmaster Mueller gave a warm smile and a nod. Father and Mother Schwartz bowed slightly as they acknowledged him sitting on the platform in the green velvet-covered chair, worn from years of use. Everyone wondered whether there would be more news about the czar's death or of his successor. Whatever the case, there was standing room only.

Karl sat down and pulled out the unfinished whistle he had stuffed in his pocket that morning. He was admiring his carving handiwork when he felt his mother's hand on his arm. Her stern look told him this was not the place to be playing with it.

He stuffed it back in his pocket and settled for gazing at the large picture of Christ hanging at the front of the sanctuary. The painting's eyes always seemed to look right through him, giving him an unsettled feeling that he'd better behave. *Why couldn't the painter have put a happier expression on Jesus' face?* Karl wondered. *At least the angel icon on the other side of the room is a little friendlier.*

The service went on a bit longer than usual. As Herr Mueller closed the sermon book, he spoke solemnly. "Evil forces are at work trying to stir up dissension among the people and the government. We must pray earnestly for God to guide our leaders and protect our freedom of religion." Many in the congregation nodded in agreement, and Amens could be heard throughout the room.

Mueller's expression lightened as he said, "We look forward to visiting at the potluck lunch following our service today. All visitors are welcome to join us. Now, let us sing our closing hymn."

The children were relieved to be set free outdoors as their parents lingered at the door with the Muellers. Seeing Edvard heading across the street to his home, Karl ran after him. He copied Edvard's steps, leaping from one small ridge in the road to the next. The last wet spell meant the wagon wheels created ruts that dried into crisscrossing spines of hardened mud, making wagon rides treacherous and difficult to manage.

"*Wie gehts* [What's going on?], Edvard? You got anything planned for today?" Karl called out.

"Not yet. But, I *have* been itching to go down to the creek and look for frogs!"

"That sounds great!" Karl beamed. "I had the hardest time sitting still today hearing the birds singing and seeing the sunshine through the window. This is the warmest day of spring we've had!"

Karl pulled out the whistle he had dutifully kept in his pocket. Edvard noticed. "Can I see it?"

"Sure, but I'm not quite done with it." Karl handed the crudely carved piece to his friend.

Just then, the last act of a dramatic performance caught his ear over by the walnut tree in front of the church. Karl spotted his nine-year-old brother Julius hanging upside down from a lower branch and teasing their sister Emma by acting as if he were going to drop her doll down to her, but then snatching it back up. This didn't last long, though, as Karl watched his towering father come up from behind Julius, grab him in a bear hug, and bring him down toward the ground headfirst, stopping just short of hitting his head.

The younger Julius's face turned from surprise to fear to laughter as he realized who had him. He instantly released the doll to a soft landing on the grass and rolled over to face his father. Knowing he had been caught in the act of teasing his sister, he jumped up and handed little Emma her doll and told her he was sorry. And all was well.

The best outcome of the whole episode, though, was that the adult conversation had been broken up and everyone was now heading for the potluck in the Muellers' yard. Baskets of food were carried from the cool shade of the walnut tree to a long, makeshift table left set up in the yard for this and other social events.

As was customary, a fence fashioned from thick sticks tethered together surrounded the Mueller yard and every other house down the street. The Mueller home, which was constructed of clay and whitewashed blocks and was covered with a thatched roof, formed the rear corner of the lot. The oldest homes were often built from wood, but the fast-growing village quickly consumed the nearby trees. Thus, the later immigrants had to get creative to build their homes and fuel their fires. There was a village corral where the cows and horses were kept, allowing smaller animals and chickens to inhabit the yard surrounding the houses.

Some of the women were already putting food on the table, ready for the hungry little ones who always waited eagerly at the head of the line. The children naturally segregated into groups of boys and girls. Unfortunate was the older sibling who had to watch over his younger brothers or sisters and miss out on the older kids' conversations. Thankfully, Karl was allowed to join the boys this time.

"Will you be back in school next week, Karl?" his friend Peter asked.

"Yes. We finished the plowing. Father will go back to plant the seed next week without us."

"Good. We haven't had enough boys to play football [soccer]."

As the last person went through line, the *kasknopfle* (cheese pockets) and potato salad quickly disappeared. The kids soon begged for the strudel (fruit-filled pastry) to be handed out.

Finishing first, Karl and his friends asked to be excused for a walk down to the creek.

"You mustn't get in the water or get muddy," many mothers said, pointing their fingers.

"We won't," every child chimed.

"And do not throw things at one another."

"OK. Thank you, *Mutter*." And off they went.

The younger Schwartz siblings watched enviously as Karl, Julius, and John walked down the road with the others.

The path the creek took was plainly marked ahead with bushes that lined its banks. This broke up the monotony of the immense Russian landscape that allowed one to see for miles in any direction. One needed only to look for the church spire to know where the next village was.

As Edvard had hoped, there were frogs galore just waiting to be caught. He quickly took off his shoes and rolled up his pants, and Julius joined right in with him.

"It's a good thing Emma didn't come along or she would run

Retribution

and tell Mama what we're doing!" Julius grinned over at Karl and John.

"Yes, but who says we won't tell on you, brother?"

"Oh, come on," Julius said. "How about the one who catches the most frogs gets out of his chores for a week? The other two have to do his work!" Karl and John looked at each other and pondered this challenge. It was one they could relish winning to see their brothers slaving away while they got a few extra winks in the morning.

"You're on!" they cried in unison, and soon all four boys were scrambling along the creek's shore, catching frogs, and putting them in makeshift pens they made with the clay soil and branches. The little frogs were too young yet to jump their way to freedom.

After an hour of hunting, the boys began to run out of frogs. Seven-year-old John ventured onto a log that bridged the creek's banks. He was halfway across when he lost his balance, toppling into the creek's deepest spot with a splash.

Karl turned quickly to see his little brother come up a few feet farther downstream. The creek wasn't that deep, but the muddy bottom made any quick movement toward John much harder. Karl and Julius somehow caught hold of John and pulled him to the creek bank. He was fine, but their clothes were another matter.

"Oh, no! We're going to get in trouble!" cried John.

"Well, what were you doing on that log, little brother?" Karl asked.

"I thought there'd be more frogs on the other side under those branches," John said.

"You were in the lead already. Just look—you have the most in your little corral." Karl pointed to the muddy pen. "Being closer to the ground evidently helps!"

Julius patted John on the back. "You did it, John! Good job. A week off from chores for you." Karl and Julius weren't so concerned over the fact they'd be doing more chores as they were over what their mother would say when she saw them.

"We better sit in the sun and dry out a bit before we go back."

"Yep. But what about the mud on John's shirt?"

Karl pondered what to do about this more obvious sign of their disobedience. "Come here, John. Take off your shirt and let's wash it in the creek and hang it up to dry." The boys' domestic abilities were lacking, and they didn't know the tricks their mother used to get such things clean. In scrubbing the shirt, they only made the muddy spot grow and soon realized they'd better stop before it got worse.

"Let's just let it dry and hope Mother doesn't notice when we get back," Karl squeaked.

When the boys returned to the Muellers', the younger children met them in the front yard. Emma noticed the shirt as soon as John emerged from behind Julius.

"You played in the creek, didn't you? You know what Mama and Papa said!"

"Emma, you know what we brought you?" Julius tried to distract her from her obvious delight in finding a way to get even for being left behind.

She eyed her brother warily and replied, "No. What?"

"A cute little frog you can have for your very own pet!"

"Really? Let me see it."

Julius pulled the captive frog from behind his back and handed it to Emma. "Now, be careful. He will jump if you don't cup your hands over him a bit."

"Oh, he's *sooo* cute! Where can I keep him? What will I feed him?"

"We'll have to get something to keep him in and go back to the creek for some water and things to eat," Julius said, with Karl and John nodding their support.

"I have to show Papa! And I'll have to ask Mama for something to put him in." Emma skipped off toward the men who were visiting in their own little group. They had gradually moved from the shade of the house out into the late afternoon sun to fend off the cool air settling in. The boys sighed with relief. They had successfully distracted her from the matter at hand, and just needed to somehow get John home to change shirts—or so they thought!

"Karl. Julius. John. Please come here!" The voice of their father was unmistakable.

The boys turned to face their retribution. They knew they were guilty, and there was no way around it. The attention they were drawing soon caused other fathers to call their boys over to inspect their clothes and question their activities.

The day's fun ended up costing the two older boys more than John's extra chores, for all three of them earned a few more chores than usual for the coming week. Ah, the lessons one must learn the hard way.

3 Young Love

The first years of Alexander III's reign as czar brought changes in the government that the citizens of Russia received with mixed reviews. He successfully broke up the terrorist and revolutionary underground, but he also tightened government control over various areas. One such change was the requirement that all schools must use the Russian language as their primary communication method.

Although the country was prospering financially, the common peasant farmer didn't see much of that in return for his hard work. The Schwartz family had been among the last German families to migrate to the Crimean region. The Turks abandoned land there, leaving whole villages empty. The Schwartzes had seized the opportunity when word reached them in Poland. Now, some years later, when word came that there was excellent land available in the warmer, fertile area of Kertch, on the southern peninsula between the Sea of Azov and the Black Sea, they packed up and moved there.

1884

The last three years had passed quickly for Karl and his family. He was now fourteen. School was something he squeezed in between gathering crops, tending fields, and harvesting. The dry, level steppes that made up most of the Crimean region where they now lived were perfectly suited to growing wheat, cotton, and garden crops. Julius Schwartz chose wheat and legumes, such as garbanzos. They also were fortunate to have a small orchard of apple trees.

"Karl, my boy," his mother said, shaking her head, "you just keep growing. You're taller than your father!"

"I know. And I'm taller than all the boys at school—even the older ones."

"I can't keep making pants for you. I'm going to make the next pair extra long, and you'll just have to roll them up to start. Now, go out and get me some apples from the cellar so I can make a *kuchen* [pronounced *cuken,* meaning "cake"]."

Karl and his brothers had become adept at handling the oxen and plow, and they could pick apples at lightning speed without bruising them. They usually had plenty stored in the cellar for the winter months. When the children could make it to school, they soaked up as much reading and writing as they could. They had to study harder because of the new laws about using Russian.

In the evenings, after supper dishes were done, Mother had everyone sit down in the kitchen. John grabbed the Bible from its place in the living room.

Mother said, "Julius, why don't you start where we left off. Where was that again?"

Julius slid his finger down where the worn ribbon marked their spot. "It's 1 Samuel 3:1."

"Good. Now, sit up and let's hear your strong voice."

Julius straightened up and began reading. "And the child Samuel ministered unto the LORD before Eli."

Mathilda, six years old, held Pauline in her lap. Karl, towering above everyone at six feet, two inches, watched the fire dancing in the open stove door. Finishing the chapter, Julius slid the Bible across the table to Karl. "Your turn."

Karl picked up the Bible, turned to his mother and said, "Mother, we never get to hear you read. Why don't you take a turn?"

She was caught off guard but smiled warmly. "No, no. You all need to remember your German. This is a good way to do it." The boys didn't know until much later that she had never learned to read, and listening was the only way she got her Bible knowledge. She would commit many of the verses to memory as she helped the children do the same.

School was more than just reading and writing. It was an opportunity to socialize and roughhouse with other youth. One October day, the last of the apples had been hauled off to the village's open market or put in the cellar for winter. But Karl and his younger brothers and sister Emma were up bright and early, for they got to go to school that day!

"I'm so excited, Mother. I've missed my friends!" John exclaimed.

"When will I get to go, Mother?" asked little Pauline.

"Oh, probably in a year or two, my dear. You'll be going soon enough. Besides, your mother needs you at home to help with the chores. They are jobs for big kids!"

Mother prepared a hearty breakfast of eggs, potato cakes, and fresh milk. Father came in from the chores long enough to bid them a good day at school. Lunches were prepared, and they set off for the schoolhouse. Mother had Mathilda to help care for Pauline and Henry, ages five and three.

"All right, my big girls and boy, let's make the *kuchen*. Today is Thursday—baking day. We also need to make noodle dough for next week's meals. Mathilda? Take Pauline and Henry out and gather straw for the outdoor oven. I'll be there in a few minutes."

"I'll race you!" yelled Pauline as she took off for the door.

Henry's little legs tried to catch up with her but couldn't. Mathilda grabbed his hand and pulled him along faster. They picked up straw in the corral area, and Henry left more on the ground on his way back than he had picked up.

At the schoolhouse, Schoolmaster Braun welcomed the Schwartz children as they entered. He understood the seasonal demands on the farmers and had learned to adjust his lesson plans to accommodate their children.

Karl took his seat closer to the rear of the classroom. Because of his height, he was relegated there so he didn't block others' views of the blackboard. Karl sat next to Gottlieb Krueger, his best friend, and Gottlieb's sister, Maria, was in front of him. Karl didn't mind this seating arrangement too much, for he had come to notice how Maria was the cutest girl in the room. She was two years younger, but either her "little sister" ways had gradually disappeared or he just didn't notice them anymore!

"Hi, Maria."

"Hello, Karl," she said, brushing her long brown hair behind her ear.

"Karl's got a girlfriend," his brother Julius sang in a sing-song voice.

"Hush, Julius." Karl glared at him.

"Hey, Karl—good to see you," said Gottlieb.

"Yes. I'm glad we're finally done with the harvest," Karl sighed.

"You'll catch up very soon, I'm sure," Maria added.

Karl blushed. He turned back to her and just smiled. He couldn't think of anything to say. Soon, the handbell was rung and school was in session. Schoolmaster Braun went over the division tables. No time for daydreaming when Karl was always playing catch-up with his schoolwork! Besides, he was heeding his father's advice that he should learn all he can so he'd have another way to make a living in case the government took away their land someday.

All twelve grades met in one room, so they all had recess together. Outside, the air was beginning to get a nip to it. "Let's play capture the flag!" called Herr Braun.

"Yes, yes—let's!" The children loved this game in which both teams tried to snatch the flag in the middle of the field and bring it back to their side without being tagged.

"All right. Karl and Johann, you are team captains. Begin to pick your teams."

Karl chose Gottlieb first, disappointed that Johann had already chosen Maria. At one point, Karl and Maria faced off in the middle of the field. "Come on, Maria!" yelled her team.

Circling around the flag, Karl bumped Maria by accident. "Sorry," he said.

"It's all right. I'm—" And Maria grabbed the flag.

"Why, you—" Karl took off after her. If he could tag her, the flag would come back to the middle. Maria's team went wild. Even with her flowing skirt wrapping around her legs, she had enough of a head start that she crossed safely onto her side of the field.

"Good play," gasped Karl, his hands on his knees to catch his breath.

Maria grinned. "Thanks!" By the end of recess, Maria's team had won by one point.

After school, Karl and his brothers were to get home to help with the chores. But lately, Karl had been lagging behind, supposedly to talk with Gottlieb.

"What do you do when you get home, Karl?" Maria asked.

"Oh, I have to feed and water the animals. Sometimes, if there's metal work to be done, Father has the fire hot and ready so I can get some work done before sundown."

"That explains the marks on your hands."

Karl looked at his callused hands with burn scars from his earlier days of blacksmithing. "Yes. That and working in the fields."

"You're lucky you get to do such fun things, Karl," said Gottlieb, who was tagging along.

"I know. Father wants us to know something besides farming."

Maria looked at Karl with admiration. But when his eyes met hers, she looked away in embarrassment. "Did you get your arithmetic finished?" Karl kicked a rock down the road with his worn boot.

"Yes," answered Maria. "But I'm not sure I got the last one right. What answer did you get?"

"I think I got eighty-one. That's what I wrote, anyway. How about you?"

"I put down seventy-two. So, one of us is wrong—or maybe we're both wrong!" Maria laughed. It was rare to see her in a foul mood.

"Are you going to the social this Saturday night?" Karl asked.

"Yeah—I am." Gottlieb interrupted. He didn't appreciate being left out of the conversation.

Karl looked from Gottlieb back to Maria. His eyes directed the question back to her.

Maria slowed as she neared her gate. "I think we're going. There isn't much else to do on a Saturday night, so it's a lot of fun when something is planned."

"I agree. Better than peeling potatoes or going to bed early." Karl was getting up the courage to ask the next question. "Well, if they have a band, would you like to dance with me?"

"That would be fun. Of course I would dance with you, Karl Schwartz."

Karl blushed. "Well, I'd best be getting on home. I have plenty to do before sundown." After saying Goodbye to Maria and Gottlieb, he took off running for home, for he had to catch up with his work and be done by supper. Homework and repairing a few hand tools would keep him busy until bedtime.

Over the past year, Karl's father had begun to teach the older boys the art of blacksmithing—partly out of necessity because they couldn't afford to replace broken tools and equipment with new ones, but also because the senior Julius was able to supplement the family's income with work that other farmers brought him.

"You're getting very good at repairing those tools, Karl," Herr Schwartz had said recently, his face glowing with pride in his oldest son. "I'm telling everyone to bring you their tools if they want them done right." Karl broke into a grin. He loved working with his hands, and he also liked pleasing his father. The work didn't bring in much money yet, but Karl earned the respect of many of the elders in town, and his family received other needed items in trade.

When Saturday night finally arrived, Karl wore his best school shirt and pants. He combed his hair back and polished his boots until they shone. He and the family arrived at the dance right on time. It was being held in the village barn that had been swept clean the day before.

"I bet Karl's gonna try to kiss Maria tonight," Julius teased.

"Really? Are ya, Karl?" asked John.

"No. I'm not," Karl snapped. "You guys just go find your friends, will you?" The other boys chuckled, and Julius punched Karl in the arm playfully. Mother Schwartz overheard the banter and couldn't help but smile.

Karl found Maria in the corner with her mother. He walked up and addressed her mother, "Hello, Frau Krueger. Nice evening."

"Yes, it is. How are you, Karl?"

"I'm very fine. Hi, Maria," he said, suddenly feeling quite warm.

"Hi, Karl."

"May I dance with Maria, Frau Krueger?"

"Why, yes. She said you had asked her. Go—enjoy yourselves."

Maria was blushing, but the dim light from the lanterns hid the pink from Karl. It matched his face, though, along with the butterflies flitting in her stomach.

The pair danced a few dances and then went back to the girls' and boys' corners of the room. Maria's friends giggled and asked her all about it, and Karl's friends teased him mercilessly. He didn't care. He was one of the few brave enough to ask a girl to dance, and he was glad he had.

4
All Grown Up

A year passed. One September morning, Father Julius couldn't leave his bed. He had finally succumbed to the nagging cough and stabbing pain behind his ribs. Therefore, someone else had to do the chores. Karl's mother, Juliana, woke him earlier than usual.

"My son," she said, her eyes dark with worry. "I'm sorry, but you must miss school today, for your father is very ill. I know how much you enjoy school, but he doesn't have the strength to get out of bed, let alone lift the pitchfork and tend the animals."

"Don't worry, Mother. The chores will be done, and I will ask Julius to recite the lessons to me later. Father must get well."

Karl slipped out of bed quietly so he didn't wake his brothers and dressed in his work clothes. He pulled on his *stiefel* (pronounced *steefle,* meaning "boots") and grabbed his *hut* off the hook by the door. Glancing toward his parents' sleeping area, he watched his mother gently wash Father's hot face with a cool cloth. *What would Mother do if something happened to him?* thought Karl. *If only we had a doctor here. God, please don't let anything happen to him. You know he is a good man. Amen.*

Karl was still outside working while the others were eating breakfast.

"Where's Karl?" asked Emma.

"He's out doing the chores."

"Why is Father still in bed?" asked John.

"He is ill. He has a fever and needs to rest. Karl will have to stay home from school. Julius, you will need to teach him your lessons tonight."

"Yes, Mother."

Juliana prepared a wild thyme and cornflower syrup for Julius Sr. This treated the chest cold pain and coughing spasms. She turned her attention to Julius. "Please keep everyone together as you walk to and from school. John and Emma, please hold Mathilda's and Pauline's hands. You'd better be on your way. Your lunches are there by the door."

"Thank you, Mother. You can count on me to keep these guys in line!" Julius replied with a grin.

"Right! He'll keep *us* in line! That's a funny one!" Emma couldn't resist the retort.

As they exited, Karl came in for breakfast. "Take some notes for me, Julius, will you?"

"Sure, brother. Maybe Herr Braun will lend me one of his books too."

"Whatever you can do, I'd appreciate it." Karl appeared ten years older than he had the day before as he sat down at the table. He dished out larger helpings than usual, for he had worked up quite an appetite from his two hours of work.

There was plenty of work to be done because Father hadn't been able to do all of his usual duties for more than a week. The milk cow needed milking, and the few head of cattle needed feeding, along with the chickens, horses, and goats. After breakfast, the scythes needed sharpening for the harvest, and a wheel needed fixing so the wagon could be used to haul the wheat back from the fields. Thank goodness Julius had taught his boys well.

Days turned into weeks, and Father still wasn't better. Julius Jr., John, and Emma had to join Karl and their mother in the harvesting. They knew what needed to be done from helping during the past few years.

"Come on, John and Julius. Let's grab the scythes and get the fields cut," Karl urged.

"And Emma and I will gather the wheat after you," Mother

All Grown Up

added. The boys, now young men, made their way across the field with their scythes, cutting down the wheat straw with sweeping motions. Mother and Emma followed behind and gathered armfuls barehanded, tying them into bundles with long, moistened straw. These would be hauled by wagon to the threshing site in town and stacked later.

At times, Mother would trade places with Julius and John, giving little Emma a much-needed break. Mother was quite adept at swinging the scythe. The work was hard, but between the five of them, the field was harvested within a week.

"OK," said Karl, sounding much like his father. "Starting tomorrow, we start the threshing." The family sat around the supper table, the fire warming the room.

"You all make me proud," Father said from his sickbed.

"Don't worry, Father. We'll get the job done," Julius Jr. said.

At the edge of town, there was a community threshing floor, where the villagers took turns threshing their harvest. A sandstone roller, between eighteen and twenty-four inches in diameter and thirty inches wide, was hooked to a yoke that the oxen would pull in a circle on the hard-packed threshing floor. Threshed wheat had to be turned over a few times in between the threshing. Then Juliana and Karl would winnow the threshed wheat so the grain would fall from the husks.

"Can I ride on the ox, Karl?" John pleaded as he watched Karl hook up the oxen to the yoke. He was going on eleven and proud of it.

"I guess that would be fine. Just keep them moving and don't let them be tempted to eat all of our hard work!" Karl sounded more like his father than his brother, but John was too excited to care. He kept the oxen about their business while his mother and brothers took a break, watching the oxen do the work for a change.

"When do you think Father will get better, Mama?" Karl

asked quietly as they winnowed the grain.

"I pray every day that God will give us our Papa back. I don't know what more we can do but pray and be patient. We don't always know what God's plans are for us. I also thank God every day for my beautiful children, and our friends who have been so helpful. You are a good son, Karl. You have made your father proud."

"Thank you, Mother. But you have all worked hard too. We will get through this, and Father will be strong again."

"I know, my dear Karl. I know."

They were interrupted as a neighbor rounded the corner, toting some of his tools that needed repair now that his harvest season was finished.

"Good day, Frau Schwartz, and Karl," he nodded in each of their directions. "I have some work for you to do, Karl."

"Very good, Herr Kurtz. What is it you need done?"

Mother called the others over to gather up the grain. Then they could get cleaned up for supper. Karl and Herr Kurtz continued to discuss the repairs and the condition of Karl's father. Karl thanked him for the work as they shook hands.

"You know, if you and your family need anything—food, help with the farm—you can call for me, Karl." Heinrich Kurtz was a crusty man, known for his stern nature among the village children. But he showed another side at this moment. He appreciated the integrity that Karl's parents had always demonstrated in their dealings, and he hoped to repay Julius Schwartz in some way during this hard time.

"Thank you, Herr Kurtz. I'm sure my father would appreciate your generous offer. We have been able to keep up with things so far, but any blacksmithing jobs I can get will help."

"Well, I will spread the word among the other villagers that you are taking more work now that the harvest is over. You do very good work, and I'm sure others will have things needing repair. Be sure to tell your father Hello for me. We all hope to see him back on his feet and leading out in church again soon."

"I will tell him, and thank you again. I should have these things ready for you within a week."

"That will be just fine. Good evening, Karl."

"Good evening, sir." Karl tipped his wool cap to the man. *He certainly isn't as mean as we all used to think.*

The evening sky quickly darkened as it did earlier and earlier at this time of year. Karl decided to call it a day, for it was too late to start up his fire for the blacksmith work. Tomorrow they would fill the bags with grain and take them to the community storage and the market. Julius and John could make most of the deliveries, leaving Karl time to do blacksmith work. But there were more winter preparations that needed to be done in the next few weeks.

Not enough daylight to get everything done. Didn't Father used to say that every winter? How did he do everything all these years? Karl picked up Herr Kurtz's tools and pulled shut the gate to the threshing area. The evening chill definitely signaled the change in seasons, and Karl pulled up his collar as he walked home. He was relieved to have the harvesting done.

Thank You, Father in heaven, for getting us through these last few weeks. I pray that my father will soon be well. Please give him strength and keep Mother well also. We couldn't make it without her, Lord! Thank You for listening. Amen.

5

Hopes and Dreams

Julius Schwartz finally began to improve. He was able to sit at the table and eat with the family, and he began to walk out to the blacksmith shed two times each day to build up his stamina. Usually, he would find Karl hard at work over the fire pit or anvil, pounding the proper shape into the metals.

The Schwartz family had much to be thankful for that Christmas, as their father was able to join them for vespers at church. Everyone gave their greetings to Julius Sr. Juliana and Karl were probably happier than anyone that he was back in the family pew. Their prayers had been answered.

Life was fairly routine for the farming community, so anything new was very welcome. One Sunday in the spring of 1886, Schoolmaster Braun made an announcement before the service began that he would like to meet with the church elders following the service. Everyone was quite curious what it was about. Julius Schwartz and the other men waited inside for the schoolmaster to say his goodbyes to the other members. When he came in, he seemed excited about something and didn't waste any time getting to the point.

"I called this meeting today because I have something important to share with you. We are going to have a visiting evangelist here in a few weeks who I've heard is excellent at preaching the gospel, and he's had big crowds at the meetings he's conducted. I would like our church family to act as host to this preacher. My family and I are willing to put up him and his wife for the weeks they will be here. I have felt God telling me to welcome them here. What do you say? Any objections?" Herr Braun smiled warmly at each man sitting there.

"How often will he preach—will he take over for you on Sundays too?" Herr Kurtz had finally decided he liked Braun, which was no small step, but he wasn't too sure about having to adapt to someone else's preaching.

"The word I have is that he would preach three times per week—Wednesday, Friday, and Saturday evenings."

"Well, then, that would probably be all right with me," replied Herr Kurtz.

"Is there anything we have to do or provide for this preacher besides a place to stay?" asked one of the oldest members of the congregation.

"There will be a few jobs, like ushering or making sure the community folk feel welcome. Oh, and this man and his wife live on the small offerings they get, so perhaps we could set up a rotating schedule for each church family to provide some food or other services for them while they are here."

Julius Schwartz shifted in his seat and spoke up. "How do we know this preacher sticks to the Bible in his teachings?"

The schoolmaster smiled. "I can only tell you that my uncle in Germany sends his praises for him. 'You won't find a more godly man,' he said. And I have been praying for our congregation, because I think we all could use a revival. This seems to be an answer to my prayers."

"Whereas I think we all would agree that you have done an excellent job as our lay preacher and spiritual advisor between our pastor's visits," replied Julius, "I, too, believe that we could all benefit from a fresh voice now and then, and you deserve to be filled spiritually too. Therefore, I will pledge my support." Julius's comment brought unanimous agreement from the others.

"I will let you know his anticipated arrival date as soon as I hear. Thank you, men, for your support." With that, Wilhelm

Braun shook hands with each of the men as they walked toward the door to join their families outside.

The word came soon that the traveling evangelist would arrive in one week. His name was Gottfried Tetz, and his wife was Katherina. They traveled by train to Odessa and by horse and wagon the rest of the way. They were relieved to experience the warm welcome from the Brauns.

The meetings began the next Wednesday evening. Karl wasn't too sure what the excitement was about. *This traveling preacher's coming just means having to sit in church more than once a week. That doesn't sound all that exciting!* He had volunteered to stay home and do more chores the first week, but both his mother and father had said that wasn't necessary. So Karl found himself dutifully sitting through each meeting. At least, this evening he could take his time tying up the horses and tending to them so he didn't have to sit through the whole meeting.

But, as he was doing just that, who should he see but the Krueger family arriving! *Hmmm. Perhaps sitting in church a few more times wouldn't be so awful,* mused Karl. *At least the view won't be too bad!*

Deciding the horses were just fine, he slipped in just as the song service was starting. His mother glimpsed his arrival at the end of their pew and she smiled. She, too, had noticed the Kruegers take a seat a few rows up and over from them.

Karl actually enjoyed singing. He took hold of his side of the hymnal with his brother John on the other. Up ahead, Maria stole a glance toward the Schwartz family and quickly turned her eyes back to the front when she thought Karl was looking her way.

Meetings were held in the schoolhouse, but if the group got much bigger than the one tonight, they might have to see about moving to the church. The word was out that this preacher knew his Bible. Pastor Tetz began this lecture with a picture of a giant image made of different metals. King Nebuchadnezzar saw this image in a dream, and Pastor Tetz explained that each of these metals represented a nation that would rule the world for a time and then fall.

The story fascinated Karl. He was impressed with the prophecies that had come true to that point, and he found himself wanting to hear more. But, before he knew it, the meeting was over. "Friday evening's lecture will be at 7:00 p.m.," Pastor Tetz announced. After prayer, he and his wife made their way to the back to say good night to each family.

Karl didn't rush to get to the wagon. He stepped out of the way of the moving line of people and acted like he had to retie his bootlace. Finishing just as Maria and her family were passing him, he joined them in line.

"Hello, Maria. Glad you and your family could make it tonight."

Maria smiled. "Thank you, Karl. We heard how good this preacher is, and Father said we should come hear for ourselves." The Kruegers were members of the Lutheran Church.

"Yeah, I guess he has been pretty interesting. I haven't dozed off yet, anyway!"

"Ha! That says something for the man!" Maria knew she could tease Karl, for she had witnessed him catching some shut-eye on more than one occasion in school. It was usually after he had worked hard in the fields the day before. He also couldn't sit still for very long without fidgeting or getting into mischief, so she couldn't pass up poking fun since he'd given her such an opportunity.

"So, are you all coming to the meeting Friday night?"

"I don't know. We weren't sure what the meeting schedule was until now."

"Well, if we both can come early, perhaps we could go for a walk before the meeting starts. That is, if you want to."

Maria felt the heat rise in her face. "I'll ask my father on our way home. If we do come, I would like to go for a walk."

"I'll be here then. I hope you will be too. Good night, Maria."

"Good night, Karl."

Julius and John made low, teasing whistles through their teeth as Karl approached the wagon. "About time you got here, brother! Saw you with your girl there. What were you two talking about, huh?" Julius loved having such ammo to use on his bigger brother.

"Nothing you would care about, I'm sure. You wouldn't know a pretty girl from a camel if she walked up and kissed you on the lips!"

"Now, boys, that's quite enough! Julius and John, you may sit up here with your father and help him drive the wagon. Karl can sit back here with his mother for a change."

"Thanks, Mother, but you didn't have to stick up for me," Karl whispered as he climbed in. He was glad his warm cheeks didn't glow in the dark.

"I know, dear. But I know those two give you a hard enough time about Maria on your way to and from school. You deserve a break now and then!" She squeezed Karl's arm and shifted baby Rudolf in her arms. Four-year-old Henry snuggled between Karl and his mother and fell asleep easily with the rocking wagon and the rhythm of the horses' hooves on the dirt road.

The wagon wasn't usually necessary in getting to and from the school from their home eight blocks away. But, for Mother to make it to the meetings, there must be a way to get the sleepy young ones home afterward. On the nights when Mother couldn't make it, Julius would walk to the schoolhouse with the five oldest children in tow. When they returned home, they always filled in Mother on what they had learned.

On Friday, Karl asked his mother to cover for him leaving early to meet Maria. He knew he could count on her to come up with a good excuse to give to his brothers. As he made his way toward the schoolhouse, Karl could see Maria crossing the street a half-block past the school yard. Picking up his pace, Karl straightened his hair a bit and checked his shirt one more time.

"Hello, Maria! I'm glad you could come," Karl called as he crossed the rutted street.

"My father said it was fine as long as we stay in the village and make it back in time for the meeting."

"Oh, that won't be a problem. Actually, my mother said the same thing! I guess there's no getting out of those meetings as long as our parents like what this man has to say!"

"Well, my folks were impressed enough last time to come again tonight. I think it's because Elder Tetz uses the Bible so much. You can't really argue with the Bible, although sometimes it's kind of hard to understand."

"Yeah. I just have a hard time listening after I've already sat in school all day. A man wasn't meant to sit that much or they would put padding on the seats!"

"Ha, Karl! So you're a man now, huh? I'd like to hear you give that excuse to Mr. Braun next time you get in trouble for leaving your seat *again*. I'm sure he would understand, being a *man* himself!" Karl steered Maria around a puddle in the pathway that paralleled the road. The conversation turned to other things, and they soon found themselves at the end of the road before it took a turn toward the docks of the Black Sea.

"Do you ever wonder what is on the other side of the sea, Maria?"

Following Karl's gaze toward the south, Maria watched the sun begin its descent below the western horizon.

"Now that you mention it, I do! I like to read about other lands, but we have so few books available. What do you think it's like on the other side, Karl?"

"I don't know. Perhaps there are forests of trees covering the land for as far as one can see. No need to worry about running out of wood for building homes and making fires. And I think there are mountains higher than one can reach in a day. I have heard there are such mountains in other places."

"I have no doubt that you will see those mountains someday. But, Karl, right now I think we'd better turn around and head back before that sun disappears!"

Karl awoke from his daydreaming to the reality of the moment. "You're right! All we need is for me to get you back late. Do you think you can run in your dress?"

"Well, I'll give it a try. Race you to the next corner!" Maria picked up her skirt and took off before Karl had a chance to think. It didn't take him long, however, to catch up and pass her, waiting for her at the corner. Laughing between breaths, the two of them ran a half-block more before conceding that they would be a few minutes late. Of course, Karl didn't mind, but he didn't want to make a bad impression on Herr Krueger.

As they made their way through the door, the people were just closing their hymnals from the last song. Pastor Tetz directed everyone to bow their heads for opening prayer. Karl took the opportunity to reach for Maria's hand, giving it a squeeze as the "Amen" was said. They parted and went to sit with their families under the watchful eyes of the adults in the room, not to mention the siblings who nudged one another and barely held in their snickers. Whatever teasing he would have to endure would be worth the time he had just spent with Maria. It was the first of many walks they would take, talking about their hopes and dreams.

6 Sabbath

"What are we going to do, my dear husband?"

Julius looked up from his porridge with upraised eyebrows. "Do about what, *meine* Frau?"

"About this Sabbath business! Do you think we have been worshiping on the wrong day all this time? How could so many scholars be wrong about such a thing? Why haven't we heard these scriptures before in this way?" Juliana Schwartz had carried a heavy burden on her heart since the evangelist's talk the Saturday before.

"Well, remember how Pastor Tetz said that the Sabbath became a political issue over power and who ran the church? The church had always told the people what to do. I have not been able to think of much else since his talk on this, either. But, let's not get too up in arms until I've had a chance to talk with the schoolmaster and the elders. We've called a meeting after lunch this Sunday to discuss things."

Juliana began clearing away her husband's dishes, stopping to look into his eyes. "I won't say any more until you and the elders have met. But, I am anxious to hear what Herr Braun has to say about this."

"*Ach,* I am also anxious to hear." Julius gave his wife a gentle touch on her arm as she picked up the last of the dishes. "Until then, we must pray that God is at these meetings and that people will not be led astray."

The next meeting's topic was a bit lighter than the previous one, entitled "The Family of God." It was something everyone could relate to—how to make your own home a place where God and His angels would happily dwell.

Pastor Tetz, aware of the elders' meeting the next day after church, seemed to indicate his own concerns in his closing prayer: "And dear Lord, please bless this community of people from all backgrounds who have joined here together to worship the one true God. We ask Your guidance in our decisions, which can make a deep impact on our daily lives, as well as on our eternal lives. May Your Spirit dwell among us, is our prayer. Amen."

At the elders' meeting the next afternoon, as Herr Braun walked to the front of the schoolroom, he sent up a quick prayer for the right words to say.

"So, Schoolmaster, what do you make of this man's teachings?" implored the town's most opinionated man, Herr Zynich.

"Yes! How dare he come here and tell us we have been worshiping on the wrong day! Why, everyone worships on Sunday, right?" joined in a few others who wanted some answers.

"Now, my dear friends, I know you have questions, but I must be honest with you. I don't know that I have the answers you want to hear." Herr Braun cleared his throat and picked his words carefully.

"I must admit that I didn't know what to make of these new teachings when Pastor Tetz shared them with me prior to his meeting about the Sabbath. We spent a great deal of time together on the subject the week before, searching the Scriptures and the life of Christ, and the reason I allowed Brother Tetz to share this teaching with you is because I am becoming more and more convinced of its relevance."

Julius could stay silent no longer. "You mean to tell us, you think Pastor Tetz is right? That the Sabbath day is to be kept on Saturday—the *seventh* day?"

"Yes, Julius, I am ready to concede that if we are to truly follow what the Bible says, we should be keeping the seventh day holy, not the first day of the week."

The silence among the elders seated before Herr Braun was louder than the discussion that had just taken place. Even Herr Zynich was speechless for the moment!

"Surely Scripture defends our worship on Sunday! You just haven't looked hard enough," proclaimed one.

"There is no command that tells us the Sabbath was changed to Sunday, the first day. I have searched my seminary books and cannot find any scriptural evidence that says the new Christians changed the day after Christ's death and resurrection. I can only believe that Pastor Tetz is correct in saying that this change occurred because of the Orthodox Church's heavy influence in past history."

"Perhaps we need to hear more from Pastor Tetz on this subject. I want to follow what the Bible says, and I respect this man, but I need to hear the evidence he has shared with you." Julius looked toward Braun as he emphasized the last part of his statement. Other elders nodded their agreement.

"Very well. I can't blame you for that. I will ask Brother Tetz if he will meet with the elders at a time that fits your schedules. Any preferences, gentlemen?"

The men discussed a time that wouldn't interfere with their regular workweek, and it was suggested they meet the next Sunday after church and lunch. They all agreed to have Herr Braun ask Pastor Tetz whether this was agreeable with him. Satisfied with the plan, the men dispersed to the school yard, where many of their wives were waiting patiently as the children played.

* * * * *

The meeting took place the next Sunday between the elders, Schoolmaster Braun, and Pastor Tetz. With the Holy Spirit's help, Pastor Tetz was able to show many of the men convincing evidence that the original Sabbath of the fourth commandment was still the Sabbath of their Lord. However, there were those, such as Herr Kurtz, Herr Zynich, and others, who could not be convinced. The meeting could have quickly turned into a great debate, but Herr Braun calmed down the dissenters with a promise that the matter would be brought to their district pastor when he came in a week. In the meantime, word about the debate spread to congregations beyond theirs, and the little Baptist church was the topic of conversation for many in the village of Kertch.

7
Against the Norm

"Father, do you ever think that maybe Pastor Tetz is wrong about this seventh-day Sabbath?" Karl sat beside his father in the wagon as they headed to the other side of town to pick up some scrap iron.

"I understand your question, my son, but when Pastor Tetz explains everything, I can't find any evidence to prove him wrong. It hasn't been as easy for me as for your mother to accept this, but I must admit that perhaps we get stuck in our ways and tend to follow tradition. If I hadn't read it for myself in the Bible, I might find it hard to follow too. But, as it is, I can no longer keep Sunday as the Lord's Day with a clear conscience."

"But, Papa, the kids at school are making fun of us. Do you think the people will ever get over our changing our day of worship? I mean, I don't understand why people who have been our friends for so long would now treat us so badly. And why would the district pastor, who knows his Bible, disagree with this teaching?"

"People do such things for various reasons—it could be that their pride keeps them from admitting they might be wrong, or they might feel guilty because they know they're wrong. Some are offended that we would choose to leave their beliefs. Whatever it may be, we must trust that God will watch over us and bless our faith."

"I'm just glad we have to work in the field again so we don't have to be at school. At least the Kruegers are also becoming Sabbath keepers—and, of course, the Muellers, the Helms, and the Brauns! I don't know whether I would have the courage to change if I were the schoolmaster."

"Yes, that did take courage and conviction. We need to pray that the townsfolk will not turn on him so that he loses his job. Thank goodness schoolmasters are not easy to come by; they *have* to keep him for now! By the way, I saw that little grin on your face when you mentioned the Kruegers. I'm guessing that it isn't just because Gottlieb is your good friend that you are pleased. Am I right?"

"Perhaps there is more than one reason why I'm glad they are joining us. But, Papa, you can't blame me, can you? Maria is a special girl."

"That she is. That she is. You make us proud in the decisions you've made over the years, Karl. You have proven yourself a responsible, hardworking young man. I will never forget how you took care of your mother and all of us while I was sick. Mother and I trust that you will let God lead in your future decisions and relationships, as you have thus far. You have my blessing on whatever comes of your relationship with Maria. I just hope you will not let the comments of others keep you from following the teachings of the Bible."

Their discussion was abruptly interrupted by a barrage of rotten apples hitting the wagon. Perhaps the real targets had been Karl and his father, but the young boys who had made the throws didn't quite have the strength to launch them that far.

"Dort gehen der Judelieben! [There go the Jew lovers!] *Juden* [*yu-den*], *Juden!"* the boys yelled in a sing-song way, drawing the attention of passersby.

Karl turned just in time to see that one of the boys' faces belonged to Hans Kurtz. His father, Emil Kurtz, was one friend who had turned against church members who were upsetting the community by following some "heretic preacher." Obviously, his opinions were being heard at home, and the children were quick to join the campaign against the "Sabbath keepers."

Following his father's lead, Karl turned his eyes toward the road in front of them, politely nodding their heads to acknowledge pedestrians every now and then. No need to retaliate against such behavior, because things would only deteriorate further, as Karl had learned at school.

Passing various storefronts along the way, they pulled up in front of a pier where materials were sold to the farmers and small industries in the village. Karl sat a moment longer than his father and stared out across the water.

I will do what I am told, but I don't like what it's doing to our friendships, thought Karl. *God just doesn't know how hard it can be. Why doesn't He just send down fire from heaven and announce what the true Sabbath is to be? Why does He put up with people doing what they please?*

Karl didn't expect a fiery answer to his questions, but he did look up at the blue sky overhead as he got down from the wagon. For now, there was work to be done. Answers to such questions would have to wait.

The meetings were coming to a close soon, and Pastor Tetz and his wife would be moving on to another village to spread their message. A baptism was planned for the last Sabbath for those who had never been baptized by immersion. Many of the Baptists, though they followed the same practice, wanted to go through it again to acknowledge their newfound beliefs.

Juliana and Julius Schwartz joined the others that Sabbath, and when the day was over, the village of Kertch had a congregation of Seventh-day Adventists—eighteen adults and twenty-seven children. They met each Sabbath in the homes of members because they were no longer welcome to use the schoolhouse.

As Karl came to realize, God *does* know how hard it is to go against the norm. His own Son had done just that, and He had had to endure much harsher treatment than Karl could ever imagine. Both he and Maria would come to understand the sacrifice that Christ had made for them, and they would choose to follow His example.

8 Proposal

Life in the southern Ukraine went on as usual for the German families, but things were becoming tense in the areas north of them. A drought had begun to take its toll on the harvests and livestock, and the country's leadership was taking more than its usual share, as a tax, to keep the bureaucracy comfortable. That left the peasants near starvation in many areas. The fertile soil near the Black Sea became an important source of grains and fruits to sustain the country during these difficult years.

1889

Between honing their blacksmithing skills in the winter months and planting and harvesting crops during the warm months, the Schwartz boys and their father worked hard year-round. The nearby shipyards brought in a little income for the large family at a time when money was hard to come by. With eight children to feed, Julius and Juliana were grateful for the contributions that anyone could make.

Karl and Julius Jr. were allowed to put away a small part of their earnings, after tithe, toward their futures, and Karl had reasons for being diligent about saving. He wanted to ask Maria for her hand in marriage, and he finally felt he had enough to provide a home for her.

Wanting the perfect time to ask, Karl obtained Herr Krueger's blessing and then waited anxiously for Christmas Eve to come around. When that day arrived, he helped his mother prepare a table for two in their small eating area, complete with candles and linens reserved for special occasions. As part of the plan, the Kruegers had invited the Schwartz family over for dinner, but Karl would somehow get Maria to go on a romantic walk beforehand.

Karl's brothers realized how important this evening was to Karl, but they couldn't let him off without some kind of gibe. "Better clean your teeth real good, Karl. You wouldn't want Maria to gag when you pop the question!"

"Thanks for your concern, my loving brothers! Remind me to bring some rope tonight. I might just have to tie you to your chairs at the Kruegers' to make sure you don't follow us back here!"

"Oh, no need for that, Karl. We aren't really interested in seeing you sweat and fumble for the right words to say. Hard to imagine our Karl speechless, though. That might be fun to watch!" Julius and John nudged each other and with triumphant chuckles scooped young Rudolf off his feet as he joined in the laughter at their brother.

After the cordial greetings given at the Kruegers' door, Maria offered to take everyone's coat to the back bedroom. When she got to Karl, he took the opportunity to invite her to take a stroll in the snow.

"Well, I don't know whether I can leave Mother to finish getting the food ready." Maria gestured toward the table set with every dish in their possession.

"Don't worry about helping, my dear. Between the girls and me, your mother has plenty of help!" broke in Juliana Schwartz.

"Mother?" Her eyes really asking the permission, Maria looked at Frau Krueger.

"I think that would be just fine, dear. Just be sure to bundle up against the cold." Looking back at Karl, Maria replied, "Well, I guess I'm not needed here, so let's go." Karl winked at his mother as Maria went to get her coat. Things were going even better than planned.

The moon glistened across the sleeping fields of old snow covered with a new coat of white. Beneath the crusty surface in the fields stood the stubby remains of the last harvest. Karl and Maria steered outside the frozen pathway to enjoy the crunch of the snow that hadn't yet been trampled. Each of them had mittens, but they had figured out a way to fit both their hands into one of Karl's so they could walk together hand in hand.

"So, do you know what you're going to get for Christmas?" Karl had rehearsed the small talk for the past few hours.

"I think Mother has been knitting some things for all of us. I could use a new sweater and some larger mittens!" She squeezed Karl's hand as she smiled up at him.

"Perhaps we could get her to knit one big one for us! But, then again, she might wonder!"

As they walked to the edge of the neighborhood, new snowflakes began their lazy descent. Held in the embrace of sacred silence, they stood gazing at the clouds sliding slowly in front of the moon. Finally, without a word, they turned back toward their families, ending up in front of Karl's home.

"We'd better hurry back, Karl. We have been gone longer than it should have taken to have everything ready." Maria pulled Karl in the direction of her home.

"Just a minute, Maria. I have something I want to show you here before we go back. Come with me." Karl pulled her back and helped her up the slick path to his front door.

Maria noticed a glow through the front window, and with a slight note of concern framing her voice, she said, "It looks like someone left a lamp burning. I hope everything is all right."

"Oh, I'm sure everything is just fine." Karl opened the door, and instead of leading the way in, stepped aside and politely motioned Maria in first, bowing at the waist.

Maria giggled at this gentlemanly act and stepped over the threshold into the front room. Within seconds, a gasp escaped

Proposal

her lips as she took in the wonderfully decorated table for two with the candles burning softly, welcoming them into the warmth from the stove.

"What is all this? Who is this for?"

"Why, for the most beautiful girl in the world, I must say. May I take your coat, madam?" Maria, in shocked silence, allowed Karl to remove her coat. She sat in the chair Karl pulled out for her and accepted the napkin for her lap.

As if on cue, a waiter—Henry—entered the room in his best pants and white shirt, and offered them tea to drink. Emma appeared from her hiding place in the kitchen and began to bring dishes of food. Henry brought a plate of *brotten* and asked if there was anything else they would be needing.

"No, thank you, Henry. You may leave us for the time being. Thank you, Miss Emma. I will ring if I need you."

Still not quite sure what to make of everything, Maria confirmed her appreciation. "Yes. Thank you very much." Henry and Emma then took their leave to the back bedroom, trying not to make any noise as they positioned themselves to watch the drama through the crack in the adjoining wall.

After the couple had taken a stab at eating enough to call it a meal and making small talk that soon ceased to make much sense, Karl gave in to the anticipation of the evening. Pushing away from the table as he wiped his mouth with the linen napkin, he reached into his pocket and pulled out a small homemade box. Getting down on one knee, he reached for Maria's hand and turned her toward him.

"Maria, in case you didn't realize it already, I have grown to love you, and I think of you every minute of the day. I hope you feel the same way about me and would consider being my wife."

Maria had been fighting the thoughts that this might possibly be what Karl was up to, so it took a moment for her to allow the reality to sink in. But sink in it did, and without reservation, she gushed, "Of course I will, Karl Schwartz! I was beginning to wonder if you'd ever ask." They embraced and, looking over Maria's shoulder, Karl could see Henry and Emma dancing a jig in the next room. He smiled and gave Maria another squeeze, then remembered the box in his hand.

"I don't have a ring, Maria, but I wanted to give you something. I hope you like it. I wanted something that would remind you of me." Maria untied the ribbon that had been saved and used many times from Christmases past and opened the box to find a beautiful brooch decorated with flowers and a border of gold.

"It's beautiful, Karl. I will cherish it forever," she said as Karl helped her pin it on. They embraced once more but were interrupted by giggling outside the front door. Seeing that they were discovered, the door burst open and a tidal wave of Krueger and Schwartz family members burst in, wanting to offer their congratulations. Maria and Karl wondered how long they had had an audience but quickly lost concern as they received hugs from everyone more than once.

9

What God Hath Joined Together . . .

The wedding date was easy to arrive at because Pastor and Mrs. Tetz were to be back in Kertch for a few days in February 1890. They would be passing through on their way to yet another evangelistic series.

The day dawned crisp and bright as the sun reflected off the five-thousand-foot peaks of the Crimean Mountains to the west. Karl couldn't take his eyes off of his bride, and if not for her squeezing his hand at just the right moment, he might have missed his cue. "And do you, Karl, take this lovely woman to be your wife?" Pastor Tetz gave a wink and a smile to the beaming groom.

"I do!" Karl replied without hesitation. Then, for emphasis, "Yes, I really do!" A few chuckles went up from the group gathered behind them.

"Very well. I pronounce you husband and wife. What God hath joined together, let no man put asunder." Karl and Maria embraced each other for the first married kiss. The couple, both blushing, turned to meet the family and friends who were already coming forward to show their support and give congratulations. Since church services were now held in the Braun home, there was hardly room to turn around, let alone set up a receiving line. The line quickly turned into a maze.

Because the wedding had become the special feature for the Sabbath School period, the sermon was yet to follow. But it took a bit for everyone to get their chance to wish the newlyweds well.

Pastor Tetz took the opportunity to preach about the Bridegroom in the Bible who will one day come to take His bride home.

Noticing his brother Julius sitting next to the Tetzes' daughter, Katherina, Maria nudged Karl to look. They gave each other a knowing grin and snuggled closer, trying hard to concentrate on the rest of the sermon.

* * * * *

Settling down in Kertch, Maria gave birth to their first child, Vernand, a year later. Unfortunately, at nine months of age, he became quite ill. Karl was heartbroken as he watched his firstborn son die in his arms. Such were the cruelties of life in those times, and Karl also lost three sisters to diphtheria that year. Their next child, born in 1892, would be named after Karl's twelve-year-old sister, Pauline, who had died. This new baby helped ease the pain of their earlier loss.

* * * * *

Karl continued blacksmithing and helping his father with the crops. One day, Maria looked out the window to see Karl trudging slowly toward the house. His feet appeared to be carrying three times their usual weight.

"Papa's coming, Pauline. See your papa, little one?" She cooed to the baby and playfully took the child's little hand to wave out the window. Not sure what to make of Karl's demeanor, Maria tried to sound upbeat. "Hello, Pauly's papa! What brings you home so early in the day?"

Karl didn't want to alarm her, but he had just come from the magistrate's office. "My dear wife, I couldn't return to my work until I had seen my girls and given them each a hug."

"Is everything all right in town? Why did you leave your work in the first place?"

"Maria, come and sit by the warm stove here, and let me hold Pauline."

They sat close enough for Karl to put his arm around Maria's shoulders and still cradle the baby.

"We—that is, I and the other men who have turned twenty-one—must register for the army." A gasp escaped from Maria. "And now we are to report for duty in four days."

"That can't be! You aren't even a native in this country! How can they make you join their army?"

"I asked the same question, but they offered no explanation other than we should be proud to defend our own people from our adopted country's enemies. We didn't think we could really argue with the man. He might have had us arrested!"

Maria began to lose her composure. Soon the three of them were crying and embracing, although little Pauline had no idea what her parents were upset about. She just knew she didn't like it and joined right in.

"Karl, what if something happens to you? What would we do?"

"Now, Maria, you mustn't think such things. We must put everything in God's hands and trust Him to take care of us."

"But why does the czar need more men in his army? He isn't at war with anyone!"

Karl shifted Pauline to his other arm and reached for Maria's chin, tipping her head back to look into her eyes.

"That is the good thing, darling. I probably won't have to do any fighting because things are fairly peaceful right now."

Maria wiped her eyes with her apron. "How long must you be away?"

"Perhaps three years or more. Longer than any man should have to be away from his family!"

Realizing how hard it would be for Karl to leave her and Pauline, Maria found within her a strength she didn't know she had. "My dear husband, we will survive somehow. You needn't worry about us. I will keep busy helping with the planting and harvesting, and before we know it, you will be back home. Everything will be fine."

"I am lucky to have you for my wife. And Pauly is even luckier to have you for her mother!" Karl lifted the child high in the air, bringing from her a giggle and a grin.

10 In the Service of the Czar

The next few months went by quickly. Maria worked hard, helping her father-in-law and the boys in the fields and helping Frau Juliana with household chores. She and Pauline had moved in with the Schwartzes shortly after Karl left, because his army pay was barely enough for his own food and necessities. Although Maria loved her in-laws dearly, there were times when she and Juliana differed on how things should be done, and Maria usually deferred to the older woman. These difficult moments only caused Maria to miss Karl more, sometimes to the point of resentment.

If Maria only knew the hardships Karl and the other men were made to endure. Life in the army did not mean you had everything given to you by the government. The average pay was forty-eight rubles ($1.40) per month, and soldiers were expected to buy their own food and clothing!

Needless to say, many men were undernourished or often became ill from eating stale, moldy bread or fruits and vegetables, not only because of the lack of money but also because of the lack of food from the famine. Breakfast consisted of bread and tea, and lunch was *borsch* (beet soup), which was placed in one big bowl surrounded by eight to ten men. Each man carried a wooden spoon, storing it handle-first in his boot.

When winter rolled around, Karl was thankful for his warm sheepskin coat and felt boots. The army officials soon discovered his blacksmithing talents. They often put him to work on the ever-expanding railroad system during the winter, instructing other men in metal work. In the warmer months, they put him in charge of the farmland that provided food for the czar, his family, and other government dignitaries. Karl quickly established himself as a leader among the men and was put in charge of ten to twelve men—much like a lieutenant—but without the rank.

Early one October day in 1894, after two years in the army, Karl and the other men noticed an unusual stirring in the officers' camp. Georg, a young man from Odessa with whom Karl had become close friends, joined him as he stoked the fire that had been smoldering overnight. "What is going on over there? I do hope they don't have a nice twenty-mile march up their sleeves for us today! Not after that hard day we put in yesterday!"

"I don't think that's what is on their minds. I overheard one of the lieutenants say something about Czar Alexander and the future of Russia, but I don't know what it's all about." Karl blew into the embers and finally got a spark to leap into a small flame.

"Do you suppose someone has attempted an assassination on him as they successfully did to his father?"

"Who knows! But perhaps we are about to find out. Here comes our commanding officer now." The two men, along with the others in their group who were standing around waiting for their morning tea, quickly snapped to attention as the officer approached.

"At ease, men. We have received some bad news from the palace. The leader of our great country has died of some strange disease, and his son, Nicholas II, is now our czar. We are to break camp immediately and head toward the capital to set up a defensive position in the event some overzealous resisters try to attack while they think things are in disarray."

"Sir, what does this mean for us—must we go north or may we stay here for the rest of our service and work on the railroad, sir?" Karl appreciated Georg's bravery at posing such a question, for he also wanted to know what the future held for his return home.

"You, soldier, are in the service of the czar's army, no matter when or where you are called. If your unit has been called to defend His Majesty, you will go. I don't know anything about your term of service. I just follow orders, as I suggest you do!" Georg stepped back from his close proximity to the officer and looked down at the ground.

"Schwartz, have your men pack up everything and be ready to leave by noon. You are dismissed." The officer turned on his heel and headed back to his camp with his chin held high.

"What do you make of this turn of events, Karl? You and I will have served two years this coming March, and we were told we would probably be going home next year."

Karl didn't know whether to respond from his leadership role or to dare react from his heart. He, too, was concerned about going farther north—many more miles from home. He replied slowly, "I know, Georg. But, unfortunately, we don't have a lot to say about how things are run around here. Perhaps when things settle down from the czar's death, we will return. Until then, I suggest we comply or face an undesirable consequence."

A pot of water was placed on the fire to heat for tea, since there was a shortage of coffee beans. The men began to roll up their sleeping mats and to pack their few belongings. Karl stood for a moment gazing off to the southern hemisphere, imagining his young wife and daughter just rising to meet the day. He still pictured Pauline as the bouncy baby who grinned whenever he entered the room, but he knew she was probably getting into mischief as she entered her third year of life.

It isn't right for her not to have her father there, Lord. I miss Maria so much too. Please keep her and Pauly well and give them courage during our long time apart. Amen.

11 Sad News

The first year without Karl was difficult, but Maria managed to keep busy and was usually too tired to worry. He had managed to send a postcard or two since he left, but the short notes didn't tell much about the conditions he was experiencing—only about the work he was doing and the places he had seen. Of course, he expressed his love and concern for Maria and Pauline and that he looked forward to being home with "the two most beautiful women in the world!" Maria cherished these communications from him more as the months turned into years, for Karl would be unable to send many more in the future.

The young mother was to endure heartache the second year of Karl's absence. Her parents, Gottlieb and Dorothea Krueger, had heard enough about America that they seized the opportunity to go there in 1893. They gave Maria and her brother Gottlieb as many of their belongings as they wanted and sold the rest to pay for the journey to America. Their two younger children, fourteen-year-old Daniel and twelve-year-old Regina, were torn between the potential for prosperity in this new country and their love for the country and people of their childhood. But most people agreed that this was probably a good opportunity, and the Kruegers decided to be brave.

The four- to six-week voyage to America took its toll on passengers in many ways. Even though everyone was inspected very closely for diseases and other reasons to keep them off the ship, the close quarters meant that one could contract any number of unnoticed illnesses. Dorothea Krueger took ill on their voyage and

Sad News

never completely recovered. News reached Maria a few months later via a returned villager who came calling one morning as Maria was tending the chickens in the yard. Derik, a young man who missed his family too much to stay in America, first related to Maria how her younger brother and sister enjoyed the ocean voyage and all the things America had to offer. He nervously babbled on about this and that until Maria finally interrupted him to ask about her parents.

"Well, Miss Maria, you see, I don't quite know how to tell you, but things didn't go quite so well for your mother on the voyage."

Maria set down the basket containing the few eggs the hen offered that day. "Yes? Tell me, what about my mother?"

Derik took his cap from his head and fumbled with it. Looking up from the ground, he answered, "Your mother, you see, she took sick before she reached America and never could get better. I'm so sorry, miss, but your mother died two weeks after arriving in South Dakota."

Maria didn't even notice Derik taking her hand. She only knew she had to be alone right then. She turned and headed for the house, giving a half-wave back at the forlorn man as acknowledgment that she would be all right. He slowly turned toward the road, pulling his cap back down on his balding head, glancing back to see Maria scoop up her child and almost stumble through the door.

This was a lot to take in such a short time. It was hard enough that her husband was away and she didn't have her own home to tend to. Then her parents and siblings moved away—far away—and she didn't know whether she would ever see them again. But now she would never see her mother again, and the reality was almost too much to bear.

"Momma, why you sad?" Pauline tugged on Maria's apron, looking up with her big, blue eyes. Maria sat down and held Pauly close, feeling her hand weave its way into her long hair.

"I don't know, my little *pushkin*. I was just thinking about how much I miss your papa, and how proud he would be of his little girl." Maria tickled Pauly's bare feet, and out came that giggle Karl loved so much.

"Mama tickle. Pauly like tickle," chortled Pauly between giggles. "Why no Papa tickle Pauly?" Feeling the lump in her throat return instantly, Maria drew her breath and sat Pauly down on her lap facing her.

"Pauly, sweetheart, your papa is away working very hard for the czar. And someday he will come home again, and he won't ever have to go away again."

"What's a czar, Mama?" Little Pauly probably didn't remember her father, and her lack of understanding of the situation was due to her youthful naiveté. *If only we all could gain back some of that innocence,* thought Maria. *If only our children could be spared the harsh realities of this world.*

Heavy footsteps on the front step interrupted their private moment, and Pauly scooted off Maria's lap to welcome the intruder, knowing those steps belonged to her grandfather. Julius had dropped his work as soon as young Rudolf had come to tell him the sad news, and he practically ran back to the house to see what he could do.

"Grandpapa, grandpapa!" cried Pauly as she reached up for the usual hug and ride on his shoulders. Having a grandchild had brought out a new side to this strong, hardworking man, and Maria was grateful to see him now.

"Pauly! How is my favorite grandchild?" Julius gave her a kiss but didn't lift her to his shoulders, turning toward Maria and asking quietly, "And how is my dear daughter?"

"Oh, Papa Schwartz. I don't know how I am. I don't know what to do, or say. I'm just numb." Maria joined little Pauline in Julius's large embrace as he softly patted her on the back. Pauly copied him by patting her mother's head.

"There, there. You go right ahead and cry. You have every reason to be numb right now. Lord knows you have been through enough these past few months, and He won't leave you now. You just have to hold on to His promises, and one day you will see why things happened the way they did."

The three stood there while Maria quietly let out her sobs. She regained her composure just as Juliana returned from the market. Maria went to her bed to lie down for a while, leaving Julius to break the news to his wife.

A few weeks later, Maria received a second communication from her father. He had married a widow woman two weeks after her mother's death. This woman had four children of her own, and the arrangement would be beneficial to both families. Maria couldn't decide whether her sadness or relief was greater at this news—sadness at the reminder of her mother's passing, and relief that her father and siblings would be taken care of. *God does provide. I just pray that He will provide me with my Karl soon,* she thought.

12 The Imperial Guard

The new czar, Nicholas, was put under close protection in the Winter Palace at Saint Petersburg. Karl and Georg arrived in the camp outside the city amid a snowstorm. They quickly bedded down and tried to get some sleep.

Their duties would begin the next day as they were divided into troops to march into the city and show the presence of the czar's powerful army. This routine would continue well into the new year. Over the next months, the talk of an uprising died down, and the soldiers were given other jobs in areas in which they were experienced. Karl and Georg ended up working in the fields, preparing them for that year's crops. There weren't enough oxen and horses to do the big job, so many men had to use their own brute strength to break up the ground and put in the seed.

One morning, not liking the confinement of the palace, Czar Nicholas decided to take a ride on horseback out to the fields. Accompanied by his Imperial Guard, he rode down the rough road toward the groups of working soldiers. Suddenly, Nicholas stopped his horse and pointed out into the closest field. "Bring me that man there—the tall one."

One of his guard turned in to the field and rode out to the man indicated. It was Karl. With a furtive glance at Georg, Karl followed the soldier toward the impressive group. His heart began to pound as he neared and saw the man in the middle of the group. *It must be Czar Nicholas,* he thought. He didn't know whether he should bow or not. He took a chance and saluted instead.

"At ease, soldier," Nicholas commanded. "How long have you been in our army?"

"This is my third year, sir."

"From where do you come?"

Karl didn't know how honest to be with the czar. He had heard stories of how a soldier's family could be used to intimidate him. So he was vague and answered, "From the south, sir. Not far from the Black Sea."

"Well, you are here now and I would like you to become one of my guard. You are of great stature, and I can see that you are not afraid of hard work. You will gather your things and ride back with Andrei here." Then he turned toward Andrei and ordered him to bring Karl back to the palace and show him to the lieutenant in charge.

Andrei saluted and offered Karl a hand up onto the back of his massive, muscle-bound horse. Karl wished he could tell Georg what was happening, but he had no chance. He hoped he could leave a note back at camp. That evening, Karl found himself sitting around a table of well-groomed soldiers with plenty of food and drink. Passing on the drink, Karl tried not to show just how hungry he really was. He looked around to see the amount of food the other men had on their plates and took accordingly.

The next day, Lieutenant Nazar assigned Karl to the rookie troops. They began each day with marching drills and then spent the afternoon training in weaponry and tactics to protect the czar and his family. Karl knew the important role the Imperial Guard played, but he wasn't completely comfortable with the duties it entailed. However, he couldn't let on for fear of the consequences.

As weeks turned into months, Karl was promoted to the mounted guard, and soon thereafter, he became the sergeant of a platoon. He became known for his strength, and also for his fairness and ability to lead. This was both an advantage and a curse.

13 A Time to Celebrate

Georg jumped into the wagon and held on as it rocked and swayed toward the city. He had been recruited to be a foot soldier directly under the Imperial Guard. He wasn't going home yet, but at least he would have a warm place to lay his head at night—and perhaps more food on his plate.

Karl noticed the wagon arriving near the stables. He didn't pay much attention until he heard his name. Georg hesitated at first. Should he make a scene? "Karl!" he called. "Is that you?"

Karl knew the voice immediately and replied, "Yes, Georg! Praise God!" He sprinted to the wagon, and the two men embraced.

Georg laughed. "You look so good—life must be treating you well, my friend. I don't know whether I should salute you or what! From your note, I didn't know whether you were going to be safe or not, going with the czar."

"Oh, I'm so sorry. I was given no time to write a longer explanation, and I didn't really know what was going to happen. We have a lot to talk about. For now, you just need to go to your barracks and get cleaned up and get a good meal in your belly. It will be nice to have you here." The men shook hands and walked to their respective barracks, smiling as they turned to make sure this was really happening. It was a nice surprise at a time when each day held new challenges.

The tone had gradually changed from the time Karl joined the guard. He had heard rumors that the government and the Orthodox Church had taken greater control around the country.

A Time to Celebrate

Attitudes toward Jewish people were becoming less tolerant. This troubled Karl because he knew from experience that his family's religious choices had sometimes been labeled as Jewish. He wondered how his family was being treated.

* * * * *

Back in Kertch, Maria was helping get the apple orchard ready for summer. Most days found them in the garden, keeping the weeds away from the sprouting plants. Pauly loved to play in the dirt.

One day, Julius came running back from a trip into town. He was waving something in his hand. "It's Karl! Karl sent a letter! Come, Maria, come!" Maria dropped her hoe, picked up Pauly, and rushed to the garden gate. Julius handed her the unopened letter.

"You don't know what it says, Father?" she asked.

"No, no. It isn't addressed to me. So hurry now and open it!" Her hands shaking, Maria opened the envelope as quickly and as carefully as possible, not wanting to tear the letter inside. It was written on rather nice paper for a soldier to have. She read:

> My dear Maria and Pauly,
>
> I do hope you are doing well and that Mother and Father are well. I am fine.
>
> Unfortunately, my time in the army has been extended again. It is so hard to believe that I have not seen you in over two years. I miss you so very much.
>
> I was reassigned in November to the czar's Imperial Guard. I really didn't do anything special to be here. I've heard he likes tall men in his guard. So, I am now living in very nice barracks within the Winter Palace's walls. My duties include guarding

the czar and his family and providing escort for them.

I am fed well and sleep in a warm bed at night. I wish for you the same. I do hope you are not suffering during these difficult times. I pray for you daily and know God has a plan to reunite us someday soon. Keep your head up and please know that I love you. Give Pauly a hug.

Love,
Karl

Maria read through the short letter again. Then she squealed, "Pauline! Papa's all right! He is safe and hopes to come home soon." She gave her a hug and set her down. Then, turning to Julius, she saw tears in his eyes. She hugged him and they did a little jig right there.

"I need to find Mother and tell her about this. Thank you, Father, for bringing home such good news." Maria took Pauline's hand and walked toward the cottage.

That evening, there was much talk and laughter in the Schwartz household. Mother Juliana brought out the much-loved applesauce she usually saved for Sabbaths and holidays. It was a happy time for everyone, and at the table, Julius said a special prayer for his son.

They still didn't know how safe Karl was. If he were that close to the czar, would he be more of a target? No one brought up such thoughts, though. This was a time to celebrate!

14 Plans

Months later

"You aren't a Jew lover, are you, Karl?" The words were practically a spit in his face, and Karl quickly thought about what his answer should be. The men were sitting around the supper table, and the subject of the Jews living in the area came up. Karl felt uncomfortable hearing some of the hateful things being said. "I think we should respect one another and each one's beliefs."

Walter, the man sitting across from him, usually didn't miss an opportunity to start a debate. He was the one who was questioning Karl.

"I personally don't know any Jews, Walter," said Karl slowly. "I just know how I would like to be treated if I were in a similar position."

"Ha! What a soft man. I don't know how you made it this far."

Karl had been very careful to speak only in Russian since he had come to the guard. He had told Georg to do the same so as not to raise questions about their loyalty to the army. Some people did not trust the Germans and didn't like that their numbers had grown in the last century.

"Ah, Walter. Perhaps my mother taught me too many manners! I'm sorry if I offended you, my friend." Karl raised his glass of water to Walter, and the gesture was returned with a hearty laugh.

After supper, Karl went outside to check on the horses. He slipped down the row of buildings toward Georg's barracks. But his attention was drawn in the other direction, where a troop of Cossacks was returning from an unknown task. These men were native to the southern part of Russia. They had come north and found good-paying jobs as the czar's enforcers of civil laws. Whenever the red-coated Cossacks approached, people would quickly turn and go the other way. They wanted nothing to do with these barbaric men and didn't want to give them any reason to get angry.

Georg was waiting for him at the designated place near the stables.

"My friend. Sorry I'm late. I couldn't get out of a table conversation!" Karl sighed.

Georg got up from the rock he was sitting on and gave Karl a handshake. "Don't worry. I just don't want you to be in jeopardy for meeting me."

"No. I don't think anyone cares if I come to visit an old friend—at least at this point. Now, what have you heard among the troops?"

"The same, except the word coming to the men from their families that things are getting harder for everyone. The czar is taking more and more from their crops, and they are supposed to worship all together in the local Orthodox Church. The schools are teaching things that are from the church, not the Bible. It is getting scary."

"So, we need to move soon. Now I'm being pressured to stay on after my four years are up to work directly for the czar. I'm afraid I'd never be allowed to leave here then," Karl said. "I have two men who want to make the break. What about you?"

"There are three more besides me who are worried about their families too. When I approached them, they were ready to leave that night!"

Karl dropped his voice. "OK. Here's what I have so far . . ."

One day, Karl had overheard two delivery men entering the grounds with their wagon after being granted entry by the guards.

They were talking in German and he heard one say, "Brother, if we could live like this, we wouldn't have to work so hard for our food." The other boy nodded and said, "Yes. But that will never happen."

Karl was not on duty that day, so he followed the wagon to its destination near the officers' meeting place. The men were delivering new uniforms that their family was under contract to make for the Imperial Guard. Karl walked up to the older boy and asked, in Russian, if he spoke Russian. The boy nodded Yes. Then Karl said quietly in German, "I, too, am German. I heard you speaking. You should be careful here. What is your name?"

The boy nodded and answered, "I am Rolf, and this is my brother, Boris. You are right, sir. We will not speak German here." Karl wanted to reassure the boys, so he asked them where their family workshop was. "We are three bridges down the river Neva from the palace, in the old section of the city. We often have to deal with the river flooding there."

Karl smiled. "I'd like to meet your family. May I follow you back on my horse?"

"I guess—I mean, yes, sir!" Rolf quickly put a positive spin on his answer. He didn't know what this soldier could want with his family, but he needed to be respectful. "I will go get my horse and meet you outside the gate." Karl turned and headed for the stables.

"So," Karl continued his story to Georg, "I went to their workshop, which is also where they live, and met the parents. Their names are Hans and Monika—very nice people. I tried to get a feel for their loyalty to Russia, as their family emigrated from Germany about the same time mine did."

"Why did you do this?" Georg was a bit confused.

"Because they make clothing. They can make us civilian clothes. And, after visiting them a few times, I discovered they are sincere Christians who also don't like the changes they see going on."

"Tell me more," Georg urged.

"Well, they agreed to make a set of clothes for each of us once they have our measurements, and I will pick them up piece by piece on my days off. They thought it would take about a month."

"Now I understand why you did what you did! Very smart, Karl. You always have been."

"The second great thing that has come out of this is that they have an aunt and uncle in a village about thirty-five miles from here, and they will probably let us stay there the first night."

Georg began to grin as excitement tinged with fear bloomed on his face. "When will we do this?"

"Unfortunately, winter will be coming in about a month or two. The question is, Do we dare go when the weather may go against us, or do we wait for spring?"

"Oh, I would be worried if we waited another six months. Many things could happen in that time. I am willing to go right away."

Karl pursed his lips. "I'm with you. I know God can watch over us. He has thus far. I'm so worried for my family, and I don't know how much longer I can be apart from them." He paused thoughtfully. "OK. Tell your recruits what the plan is, but don't tell them it will be in a month or two. The less they know, the better."

"All right. I'd better get back. We've been out here longer than usual. Take care, my friend." Georg patted Karl on the back.

"You too. I will need those measurements as soon as possible."

The men parted, each squelching his excitement upon arrival back in the barracks. Karl had a hard time getting to sleep that night.

15
Escape

The defectors quietly stuffed their beds and grabbed their pillowcases full of personal things, clothes, and a little food. The night was crisp, and they could see their breath as they crept to the stable. Karl and Georg silently signaled to their men to saddle up. They all had their uniforms on so they could say they were on a special patrol if asked. Karl had a back way to get out of the palace grounds, but there were always guards patrolling.

Everyone was silent and alert in the darkness, the night sky providing only a sliver of moonlight. They soon arrived at the back gate, and no one was nearby—their first hurdle was an easy one. Now came the most important part of the escape—getting out of the city and on their way without stirring suspicion. Karl stayed at the back of the line of men so his uniform of higher authority wouldn't be as visible. The foot soldiers led the way with directions Karl had provided earlier in the week.

A light snow began to whiten their uniforms as they made their way down backstreets and finally outside the city. They stayed off the main road, using old animal trails instead. Hoping to get as far as possible on the first night, perhaps to the family of their clothes makers, they kept up a steady pace. After a couple of hours, the snow began to fall harder. Thankfully, they had brought their winter gloves, but they couldn't bring their outer coats, as that would raise too many eyebrows.

Back at the palace, men in both barracks slept soundly. It wasn't until morning when everyone was reporting to breakfast that someone asked where Georg, Erik, Alex, and Rolan were. In

Karl's mess hall, they were looking for Viktor and Marc. What everyone found was a bed stuffed with clothing and blankets. At first no one understood and thought it might be a prank. But when the lieutenant from Karl's Imperial Guard regiment went to inform Karl in his private quarters, he found another stuffed bed. When they all compared notes, the alarm was sounded. Soldiers were on the run! And one was their own sergeant—Karl!

Meanwhile, as daylight lit the runaways' path, they were slowed a bit by the snow. They thought maybe they could use the main road for a little while since they were about seventeen miles outside the city. Almost as soon as they entered the main road, a lower-ranking soldier driving a wagon full of ammunition passed. The men held their breath. But the soldier saluted Karl and kept right on going.

This was too close of a call. Deciding to change out of their uniforms, they returned to the back trails and looked for an inconspicuous place to change. There weren't many trees to hide behind because most had been cut down to build the great city of Saint Petersburg. They finally found a ditch embankment where they were able to duck down and change their clothes, burying their uniforms in the dirt and under rocks.

Stopping now and then to rest their horses, Karl asked the men from Georg's unit a little about themselves. Each man had a family to return to and had various reasons to fear the tension building around the country. Two of the men were less than a hundred miles from home, while Karl had almost a thousand miles to cover.

Continuing on, the day gradually faded to evening. They were close to their destination for the night. Hans and Monika's uncle did not know they were coming, but Karl carried a note from them that introduced the men as friends. He hoped they wouldn't be alarmed at their arrival.

Back at the palace, the search for the men was in full force.

Escape

Walt, who had always given Karl a bad time, led a group of soldiers around the perimeter of the grounds. They came upon some hoofprints in the mud around a back gate and counted six or seven horses. They figured that this must be their escape route. Walt and the others quickly rode back to the officers' quarters to report to the other sergeant in charge.

Next, the word had to be brought to the czar. This was not something Sergeant Petroff looked forward to. But defectors were a serious matter, and Czar Nicholas must be told.

"What? They're missing? And one of them is Karl? This can't be. He is one of my most trusted guards! Are you sure?" Nicholas was shocked.

"Yes, Your Highness. We have searched the grounds, and there are seven horses missing. Hoofprints have been found near the rear gate. They probably have a seven-hour head start on us. What is your desire, sir?"

"I can't believe this. Where would they go? Home? Don't they think we will find them?" Nicholas's voice rose in intensity. "Summon the Cossack general at once! I will have his men hunt them down. This is treason! They must be killed!"

The Cossacks were given the job of finding the deserters. They mounted their horses immediately and took off down the trail leading from the back gate. Last night's snow might be helpful in the search.

16 Red Coats and Scimitars

1896

Karl dismounted his horse and went to the door. Knocking softly, he soon heard footsteps. It was Hans's uncle, Eugen.

"Wie gehts? Ich bin ein Freund mit Hans und Monika," Karl said in German. ("How are things? I'm a friend of Hans and Monika.") Uncle Eugen returned the greeting, and Karl handed him the note from Hans.

He read it quickly and smiled. "Come in! You must be cold and hungry, my friends. We have some leftovers from supper. You may take your horses to the barn, and we will get the food ready." Eugen's wife had joined them at the door. She nodded after reading the note.

The men took off the saddles and gave their horses hay and water before returning to the house. It was a relief to be in a safe place. They were happy to have a warm meal too. Soon they were laughing around the table and getting to know Eugen and Evangeline. After an hour or so, they went out to the barn to retire for the night. They needed to get up very early to get a good start the next day.

The dark night did not deter the Cossacks. They rode behind the leading man who held a torch. Now and then, they had to stop to search the area for more tracks if the trail went cold. They really had no idea what destination Karl and the men had in mind, but so far they were heading south.

Because it was no longer snowing, they made good time. About five hours later, they came upon an area with small farms.

The tracks couldn't be easier to follow! They seemed to be heading for one farm in particular. As the Cossacks got closer to the farmhouse and barn, the leader motioned for them to stop. He sent two men around the back of the house and the other three around the back of the barn. They met up on the other side of the yard.

What they found were tracks leading right up to the barn. There were men's footprints too. The Cossacks had to be quiet as they discussed what to do.

Meanwhile, in the barn, some of the horses began to stir and murmur. A few of the men awoke and listened closely. As the horses became more agitated, the men woke the others and they all took cover, most burrowing into the hay pile in the corner. Karl looked around and decided to shinny up to the crossbeams above. In the darkness, all he could hear was the other men's whispers gradually fade.

Then, Karl heard noises outside the barn doors. Horses' hooves reverberated on the half-frozen ground much like they would on a cobblestone street. Orders were given to surround the barn and watch for anyone escaping.

Oh, God, what do we do now? prayed Karl. *They'll know we are here because of our horses, and there's no way out. If we don't make it, please take care of my dear Maria and Pauly.*

Drawing in his breath so as to keep very still, he tried to align himself with the edges of the beam on which he was lying, twenty feet above the floor. He knew his friends below could also hear the voices and that they also were well aware of the impending possibility of discovery.

The double doors flew open, and six red-coated Cossacks charged in with their scimitars drawn, ready to attack. A torch was brought in, and it was all too obvious that more than a few people had been sleeping there recently. Seven horses whinnied and snorted in the stalls, and Imperial Guard saddles were piled along the wall.

Karl watched them look at one another and silently motion toward the hay. *Did they hear something? Did someone move? What are they going to do?*

The next events happened so quickly and were so horrifying that Karl's reality was confused by the laughter and joking of the red-coated men. At last, they left the barn, their sharp scimitars dripping with blood. Karl squeezed his eyes shut as hard as he could, wishing desperately to shut out the hideous scene he had just witnessed. It didn't help. He didn't dare leave his perch, or he, too, might suffer the fate of his fallen brothers.

After more than an hour, when he was sure the Cossacks were gone, he inched across the beam to the wall where he could climb down. Hearing a moan from the pile of hay, he crept toward the sound and whispered, "It's Karl. Don't be afraid." Brushing the hay away, his hand revealed someone's face. It was Georg. Karl carefully dragged him out of the hay.

"Georg—what can I do for you? Tell me what to do."

Georg could barely speak. Karl had to lean close to hear him whisper: "It's bad, Karl. I don't think I'm going to make it. It hurts so much."

Since the Cossacks had taken the horses and no more sound came from outside, Karl decided they were gone and not coming back. He ran to the house and awakened Eugen. Lighting a lantern, Eugen returned to the barn with Karl. Georg lay at the edge of the hay, gasping for breath.

"Georg, Georg! Stay with me." Karl knelt down at his side and turned to Eugen for affirmation. "Maybe we can get a doctor?"

"No," Georg whispered. "Everything will be all right. Just do one thing for me, Karl."

"Yes—anything!" Karl gasped.

"If you find my wife and sons, please tell them I love them so much—that I will see them in heaven someday." Within minutes, Georg's body went limp. He was gone. Karl and Eugen spent a moment in prayer, then stood in silence.

Turning their attention to the rest of the men, a search of the hay pile confirmed that Karl was the only survivor. A wave of devastation crashed over him, and he felt his eyes begin to burn with tears. He felt that this was all his fault.

Karl was invited to stay in the house for the next few days. He slept fitfully at night, begging God to tell him what more he could have done. Eugen and Evangeline tried to reassure him that there must be a reason why he was spared!

Knowing he would endanger his hosts if he stayed much longer, Karl told them of his plan to move on. Eugen insisted that he take one of their horses. Karl could see that he wouldn't take No for an answer, so he pulled out some money and said, "The least I can do is pay for the horse! Thank you so much for your care and the risks you have taken."

"This is what God intends us to do—help one another," Eugen smiled. "Now you need to go to your family. They will be so happy to see you. You have a long journey ahead of you. I wish you Godspeed and a fast trip. But before you go, you should leave your identification for me to plant on one of the men so they will think you perished too."

The two men embraced and then Karl mounted the horse. Evangeline reached up with a knapsack of food, and he thanked her. He rode toward the south and never looked back.

17

Walter and Anna

Karl tried not to ride his gift horse too hard, for the mare had seen better days—a far cry from the excellent mounts he'd used in the czar's Imperial Guard. On a good day, the two covered about thirty miles, but more commonly, twenty. After three weeks of almost constant travel, the poor horse just gave out. Karl found a stable willing to give him a few rubles for her, and he took off on foot. Nights were spent in kind farmers' barns or on a bed of leaves. Karl was thankful for the blanket Uncle Eugen had given him.

If Karl had looked in a mirror, he would have wondered who the man was staring back at him. His hair and beard grew longer every day. The clothes on his back were so dirty and wearing so thin that he often walked with the blanket draped around his shoulders. Peasant women picking up sticks would move to the other side of the road when they saw him coming.

The money he had been saving for the past year was running low. In his tenth week of travel, he reached Kiev in the Ukraine region, just over 650 miles from home. Emerging from the outskirts of the city, he came to the wider cobblestone streets steaming from the afternoon sun that had broken through the clouds.

He had a mission here this day. Georg's wife and children lived somewhere on the south side of the city, and he needed to bring the news of Georg's death, hard as that would be. During their time together, Georg had given Karl clues as to where to look. He had mentioned they lived along the river and that his wife ran the market next to their home with his parents. His last name was Krenz.

He rounded a corner where a group of men was emerging from a pub. They were in uniform, and Karl's heart skipped a beat. He was too close to just turn around without drawing attention, so he started to cross the street instead.

"Karl? Is that you?" a voice called out.

Karl froze, then turned slowly.

"Karl! It *is* you. What are you doing here in Kiev?" The man's uniform jacket was open, his shirttail was hanging out, and his voice was slurred from too much drink.

"Boris. Boris Rusikov. What a coincidence," said Karl, forcing a smile.

"Yes. What brings you to Kiev? Aren't you up in Saint Petersburg these days?"

"I have been, but—" Karl had to think fast. "I got my release and am on my way home."

Boris put his hand on Karl's shoulder. "Well, aren't you the lucky man! But you look terrible. I should buy you a drink in celebration. Ah, but you don't drink, do you?"

"No. I don't. Thanks, though. It was good to see you, Boris."

"Wait a minute—the last time I saw you, you were riding off with the czar. How did that turn out?"

Karl had started to walk away, but turned back. "Well, I worked at the palace for the last two years. It was an experience."

"I bet. Kind of a cushy job, I would think." Boris's demeanor had changed. "Not like the grunt work we were stuck with half the time."

"Well, Boris, I need to be on my way. Best of luck to you." Karl turned away again.

"Yeah. I'll take some of your luck. Did you leave me any, Karl?" Boris's voice got louder and seemed to be following Karl.

Karl walked faster and didn't look back.

Just what I was afraid of, thought Karl. *Of all the people to run into, it had to be Boris, the loudmouth. I hope he won't remember this when he sobers up.* He turned down the next street and made several more turns just to distance himself from the soldiers.

Back to his mission, he stopped a delivery wagon and asked the driver whether he knew of a market on the south side, near a river.

"Ha! A market near a river," the man chuckled. "In case you hadn't noticed, there is a big river that goes right through the city from north to south. You could be talking about a number of markets, man."

Karl felt a pang of disappointment, but then thought to say, "Well, it is owned by the Krenz family."

"Oh! Well, you should have said that to begin with. The Krenz market is in the Darnytsia borough, to the southeast. If you are in the general area, someone can direct you."

"Thank you, sir. You've been a great help." Karl shook his hand and felt a surge of energy.

He was hungry but hoped he could hold out until he got to the market, as his supplies were dwindling. Shifting the satchel from one shoulder to the other, he walked east until he reached the Dnieper River. He then followed the river down the boulevard bordering it.

The sun dipped low in the sky, but he knew he had to be close. Again, he stopped a man in the street. "Do you know of the Krenz market in Darnytsia?"

The man grinned widely and said, "Why, yes. You're only a few blocks from it. Just follow this street, and it will turn into a dirt road. In another block you will come upon the market."

"Thank you, thank you," Karl smiled gratefully. Relieved, Karl picked up his pace. Sure enough, the market was down the road on the right. Karl could see an older man covering the produce and a younger woman shuttering the place.

"We are closing, but if you hurry you can get something." The man glanced over his shoulder as Karl approached.

"I'm actually looking for someone. Do you know Anna Krenz?"

The woman stopped short and turned toward Karl. "I'm Anna. Why?"

"Who are you?" the man said defensively and stepped between Karl and the woman. "I am Karl Schwartz and I served with Georg."

"Georg? My Georg? How is he? Where is he?" Anna blurted.

"Well, I have difficult news for you." Karl's voice dropped as he looked down. "Georg has been killed."

The woman put her hand to her mouth. "He's dead?"

"Yes, I'm afraid so."

Her shoulders began to shake as the tears flowed. Her father-in-law put his arm around her and asked, "But how? There is no war going on."

"We were running away from the army, and the Cossacks caught up with us. They killed Georg and all the other men."

"But how did you survive?" the man asked.

Karl told them the sad story. "Georg wanted me to find you and tell you how much he loved you and his family."

"Oh, Georg. My Georg. I was afraid I would never see him again," cried Anna.

"I brought you the book he always carried with him."

As he handed it to Anna, she smiled through her tears.

"It's our book of poetry. We used to read it to each other. Thank you, Karl. You must have been a good friend to Georg."

"Yes. He was a good man. I will miss him."

"We all will," the elder Krenz said solemnly. "I must tell my wife about Georg. But you look like you could use a hot meal. You will eat supper with us and tell us more about our son. I insist."

"Well, I would greatly appreciate that, sir. Thank you."

Karl relished every bite, along with the *brot,* as they ate in silence. Gradually, the conversation picked up as they reminisced about Georg and the life he had lived. Walter Krenz remarked, "I'm so glad Georg had a good friend like you. It's obvious he trusted you and that he wanted to be with his family so much that he took the risk of leaving the army."

Karl nodded in agreement. "He talked about you all every chance he could. I'm so sorry he isn't here." Karl stared into his bowl, fighting back tears.

"Don't blame yourself," Walter said as he reached for Karl's shoulder. "You must have a purpose in this life, Karl. Don't squander it."

"Oh, I won't, sir."

"Now, you will stay here tonight, and tomorrow you will get on the train for home."

Karl shook his head. "No, I'm afraid that isn't possible. I figure I'll get home on foot in about two weeks."

"Not if I have any say in the matter. Georg's mother and I want you to get home safely and soon. We will purchase your ticket, and we won't take No for an answer."

"You are too kind. I thank you so very much," Karl replied.

18 Home

The next day, Herr Krenz took Karl to the train station. He had tried to give him new clothes, but Karl was quite worried about looking too much like his old self. Clean clothes were all he needed. The disheveled look of his hair and beard was a little less offensive now that they were clean.

The clerk at the depot looked Karl up and down as he handed Herr Krenz the ticket, who immediately gave it to Karl. "Here you are, Karl. And, here is a satchel of food my wife insisted you take. You'll need it, as the trip takes a few days. Much better than walking, though."

"Oh, yes," replied Karl. "I can't thank you enough."

"This is our thank-you for giving Georg freedom, if only for a short time. I hope you have a lovely life with your wife and child. How old would your daughter be now?"

"I guess she would be four. Hard to believe. She won't even know me, I'm afraid." The train whistle blew, and Karl shook Walter's hand. "May God be with you, Herr Krenz. I really appreciate this."

"You are welcome. Godspeed, my friend."

Karl chose a train car filled with women and children, hoping it would deter any soldiers from settling nearby. One mother moved to another seat when she took one look at him, which was fine by him. The next seventy-two hours couldn't go any slower as Karl neared home. He took the opportunity to catch up on his sleep, not even noticing the crying babies.

Early on the fourth day, Karl was awakened by the sound of

brakes. He looked out the window to the familiar landscape of Kertch—home. The train hadn't even come to a complete stop when he jumped from the steps and walked briskly down the familiar road toward home.

The town was busier than ever, with wagons being loaded with supplies, shop owners opening their doors, and everyone seeming to enjoy the sunny May day.

These last few miles were easy, compared to the long journey Karl had made. His thinner frame made him light on his feet, and he made good time. About ten o'clock in the morning, he walked down his lane and saw activity in his yard. It was Maria chopping wood. Little Pauline was playing with her doll on a tree stump.

Karl started whistling a happy tune and walked through the gate. Maria looked his way, dropped the axe and ran to Pauline. She scooped up the child and began to run toward the house.

"Maria! Wait! It's me—Karl!" Karl stopped so as not to alarm her further.

"Karl?" Maria turned and stared at this stranger before her. "Is that really you?"

"Yes, my dear. It's really me. Bring me my daughter, Pauly. I've missed you both so."

That was all he needed to say. It really was her husband! She ran back to him, and they hugged tightly with Pauline between them. But, this was all a bit much for the child, and she began to cry. Maria set her down and knelt before her. "Pauly, dear, this is your papa. Remember the stories I've told you about Papa Karl? He just looks like Saint Nicholas right now."

"Yes, Pauly. Don't be scared, honey," Karl assured her. The trio walked hand in hand into the house. Soon Karl's father and mother entered, hardly believing their eyes. Their son was home!

Karl spent the next hour or so explaining his escape from the army and the journey he had made. He avoided the scary details of the escape so as not to alarm everyone. "My next order of business is to get cleaned up so our daughter isn't afraid of me," Karl chuckled, tousling Pauly's hair.

"Yes, that would be good—not that I don't think you're handsome anyway—but let me draw you a bath, son," said Juliana.

Maria found some of Karl's old clothes and was shocked at how much weight he had lost. He decided to keep a short beard, so he wouldn't look so gaunt, not to mention the slight disguise it would give him.

Karl had had a lot of time to think about the next steps he and his family may have to take. He couldn't be sure the czar wouldn't track him all the way back to Kertch. Not only had he not fulfilled his six-year stint in the army, but he had run out on the czar himself. Just the fact that the Cossacks had come looking for them was proof the czar was not happy. Leaving his identification behind was good, but it would take only one person to spoil the ruse.

19 A New Home

Karl had been home a week and couldn't get enough to eat. Maria was so relieved to have her husband back that she couldn't stop smiling. But she noticed something different about him.

"Karl, is there something you haven't told me? You seem preoccupied."

Karl took a moment to answer her. "I guess I have been far away from here, haven't I? I'm sorry. It's just that a lot has happened these past three years."

"You know you can tell me anything, right?"

"I know." He paused. "There is something I've been putting off saying."

"What is it?" Maria reached for his hand.

"I think we should consider moving soon—to a place where no one knows us and where the army won't pass through."

"Move? Why?"

"I'm just worried there may be a price on my head. The czar sent the Cossacks after us, and people around here may talk too much." Karl squeezed her hand.

"Oh, my. I didn't know you were in that much danger. Do you really think they could come here and take you away again?"

"It could be worse than that. I'm sure the price for defection is death."

Maria gasped. "Well, then we must leave here. But where would we go?"

"I've thought about it and I think we could settle in Murzabek, Crimea. It's about ninety or so miles from here, and it's still in a

A New Home

fertile region where we could grow crops or fruit, and, perhaps, I could do some ironwork again."

"Have you told your father yet?"

"No, I wanted to talk to you first. I don't know whether they will want to come with us at their age, but that's up to them."

"Let's pray about it right now," said Maria.

"Yes—we should," Karl agreed.

The pair proceeded to pray earnestly, hand in hand. When finished, they sat in silence for a time, each deep in thought. Finally, they were interrupted by Julius coming inside. Maria excused herself and left Karl to talk with his father. In the next week, plans were finalized for Karl and Julius to make a trip to Murzabek to research the area and opportunities.

The first day of June dawned bright and clear. The men saddled up the horses and had food and bedrolls packed. They would make better time this way than with a wagon.

The village of Murzabek was nestled against a small rise in the landscape. Karl had taken note of the farmland nearby but was most intrigued with the orchards on the other side of town. Stopping at a stable, the men dismounted and let their horses drink from the trough.

"Where you hail from?" A raspy voice filtered through the crooked, sun-damaged door of the shoddily built barn.

"We are from Kertch," Karl answered. Out came a middle-aged man bent at the waist. He had a slight limp, but his grin was a welcome sight.

"Kertch. Well, you're a bit out of the way. What brings you our way?" he asked.

Julius and Karl had prepared their story beforehand. "We are looking for room to stretch. Kertch is getting too big. Pretty soon it'll have those steam-engine contraptions making noise all over the place. We like peace and quiet."

"You've found the place, then. Is it just the two of you?"

"No, there are six of us. My oldest son Karl here, his family, and my wife and youngest son."

"Sounds like you'd be interested in the Farbers' place," the man gestured east of town.

"Is it available?" Karl asked.

"They went to America. Last year. Had an opportunity and didn't even wait to sell it. Their parents are overseeing it."

"Well, we'll have to look it over," Julius said. The men got directions to the Farber property and, after stopping for a bite to eat, rode to the orchard side of town. Karl tried to contain himself as he stopped in front of a house overgrown with weeds.

Could this really be meant for us? he thought. *Lord, is there work enough for me here? Can I provide for my family?*

"You'd have your orchard, and see the shop there. It might be perfect for your anvil and fire." Julius's enthusiasm was rising, just like Karl's.

"Yes. It does look good so far. Let's walk around a little more," Karl suggested. They found the door unlocked and went inside. The house had been added on to once. It had good space for a growing family. Karl felt a tingle run through him at every turn. This really seemed to be the answer to their prayers.

20 Land of Freedom

Upon their return, Karl and Julius prepared to sell the property in Kertch. It took only a month to sell it to a family who had outgrown their home in the city and wanted some land to cultivate.

A month later, all the essentials were packed into the two wagons, and the families took off for their new home. Maria had not been feeling well the last week, so the trip was not very pleasant for her. In a few weeks, she would discover that she was expecting their next child.

The year 1897 brought the birth of Lydia, and within months, Maria was pregnant again. Sadly, they lost the next baby, Daniel, but were blessed with another son, Julius, in 1899.

Before Karl had gone into the army, his brother Julius had ventured to America with his new wife. Julius's letters told of great opportunities and the freedom to worship as they pleased. Karl's wanderlust and continuous concern for the safety of his family began to eat at him. He talked with his father one fall day.

"Father, I've been thinking about America. What would you think if we went there?"

Julius hesitated only a moment as he said, "I think you need to go where your heart beckons and the Lord calls. If it is America, then so be it. You have your brother Julius there to help you get a start."

"Yes, I've thought of that. What about you and Mother? Who would take care of you?"

"Oh, you mustn't worry about us. We will manage with Rudolf here."

"Well, I will bring it up to Maria and see what she says. Thank you for your support, Father. It would be hard to leave you and Mother, but I think we must go soon if we are going to go at all."

That night, Karl talked to Maria. She wasn't shocked at the idea. She saw how Karl lit up with each letter from his brother. She had two babies and Pauline to worry about, but Karl was a great help. She kept a positive spirit most of the time, for which Karl was ever grateful.

The metalwork business had been good for the past few years, and the orchards had produced a bumper crop. Karl had saved a good amount in rubles, so the ship's passage was covered. Julius had reported that land was available in North Dakota near him, so they had a destination.

By March 1900, they had placed their most prized possessions in trunks and made the trip by train to Bremen, Germany, where they would sail for America on the ship SS *Hannover*. The three-week trip took them to the port of Baltimore, Maryland.

Another train trip to North Dakota, and the Schwartz family began a new life. Nine more children were born to Karl and Maria. They faced new hardships, but their lives were richly blessed in the land of freedom.

Epilogue

The sad reality in Russia at the beginning of the twentieth century was that life was hard and the people suffered many hardships.

Julius and Juliana were caught up in the ravages of World War I. There was a food shortage, and what food could be found was most often pillaged by soldiers on both sides of the war. Also, disease was reaching pandemic proportions. Millions were dying of typhus.

The Russian economy was devastated, with factories and bridges destroyed, cattle and raw materials pillaged, mines flooded, and machines damaged. Houses were crumbling.

There were three sons now in America—Karl, Julius, and Henry, all of whom felt helpless knowing their parents were suffering. But Julius and Juliana weren't willing to leave Crimea. It was hard to hear of their passing in 1919.

Karl's daughter Leah eventually married Adolph Knittel, whose parents, Adolph and Carolina Werner Knittel, also came from Russia in 1885. Adolph and Leah Schwartz Knittel are my husband, Monty's, grandparents.

Karl eventually moved his family to Farmington, in eastern Washington, where he and Maria are now buried. Their descendants number in the hundreds. They have inherited Karl's exceptional work ethic. Some remain in the family business —agriculture—using modern equipment to farm thousands of acres in a way that Karl could have only imagined. Others have gone on to earn degrees in some of the nation's finest universities, to become health care professionals, teachers, lawyers, administrators, and pastors. They have spread their wings in countless ways to help others in time of need through mission trips across the globe and local community involvement.

But most of all, Karl's modern family has remembered his commitment to following God's Word and seeking His will in all they do.